Thomas Hardy's Major Novels

THE MAGILL BIBLIOGRAPHIES

The American Presidents, by Norman S. Cohen, 1989
Black American Women Novelists, by Craig Werner, 1989
Classical Greek and Roman Drama, by Robert J. Forman, 1989
Contemporary Latin American Fiction, by Keith H. Brower, 1989
Masters of Mystery and Detective Fiction, by J. Randolph Cox, 1989
Nineteenth Century American Poetry, by Philip K. Jason, 1989
Restoration Drama, by Thomas J. Taylor, 1989
Twentieth Century European Short Story, by Charles E. May, 1989
The Victorian Novel, by Laurence W. Mazzeno, 1989
Women's Issues, by Laura Stempel Mumford, 1989
America in Space, by Russell R. Tobias, 1991
The American Constitution, by Robert J. Janosik, 1991
The Classical Epic, by Thomas J. Sienkewicz, 1991
English Romantic Poetry, by Bryan Aubrey, 1991
Ethics, by John K. Roth, 1991
The Immigrant Experience, by Paul D. Mageli, 1991
The Modern American Novel, by Steven G. Kellman, 1991
Native Americans, by Frederick E. Hoxie and Harvey Markowitz, 1991
American Drama: 1918-1960, by R. Baird Shuman, 1992
American Ethnic Literatures, by David R. Peck, 1992
American Theatre History, by Thomas J. Taylor, 1992
The Atomic Bomb, by Hans G. Graetzer and Larry M. Browning, 1992
Biography, by Carl Rollyson, 1992
The History of Science, by Gordon L. Miller, 1992
The Origin and Evolution of Life on Earth, by David W. Hollar, 1992
Pan-Africanism, by Michael W. Williams, 1992
Resources for Writers, by R. Baird Shuman, 1992
Shakespeare, by Joseph Rosenblum, 1992
The Vietnam War in Literature, by Philip K. Jason, 1992
Contemporary Southern Women Fiction Writers, by Rosemary M.
    Canfield Reisman and Christopher J. Canfield, 1994
Cycles in Humans and Nature, by John T. Burns, 1994
Environmental Studies, by Diane M. Fortner, 1994
Poverty in America, by Steven Pressman, 1994
The Short Story in English: Britain and North America, by Dean
    Baldwin and Gregory L. Morris, 1994

Victorian Poetry, by Laurence W. Mazzeno, 1995
Human Rights in Theory and Practice, by Gregory J. Walters, 1995
Energy, by Joseph R. Rudolph, Jr., 1995
A Bibliographic History of the Book, by Joseph Rosenblum, 1995
The Search for Economics as a Science, by the Editors of Salem Press
　　(Lynn Turgeon, Consulting Editor), 1995
Psychology, by the Editors of Salem Press (Susan E. Beers, Consulting
　　Editor), 1995
World Mythology, by Thomas J. Sienkewicz, 1996
*Art, Truth, and High Politics: A Bibliographic Study of the Official
　　Lives of Queen Victoria's Ministers in Cabinet, 1843-1969*, by John
　　Powell, 1996
Popular Physics and Astronomy, by Roger Smith, 1996
Paradise Lost, by P. J. Klemp, 1996
Social Movement Theory and Research, by Roberta Garner and John
　　Tenuto, 1996
Propaganda in Twentieth Century War and Politics, by Robert Cole,
　　1996
The Kings of Medieval England, c. 560-1485, by Larry W. Usilton, 1996
The British Novel 1680-1832, by Laurence W. Mazzeno, 1997
The Impact of Napoleon, 1800-1815, by Leigh Ann Whaley, 1997
Cosmic Influences on Humans, Animals, and Plants, by John T. Burns,
　　1997
One Hundred Years of American Women Writing, 1848-1948, by Jane
　　Missner Barstow, 1997
Vietnam Studies, by Carl Singleton, 1997
British Women Writers, 1700-1850, by Barbara J. Horwitz, 1997
The United States and Latin America, by John A. Britton, 1997
Reinterpreting Russia, by Steve D. Boilard, 1997
Theories of Myth, by Thomas J. Sienkewicz, 1997
Women and Health, by Frances R. Belmonte, 1997
Contemporary Southern Men Fiction Writers, by Rosemary M.
　　Canfield Reisman and Suzanne Booker-Canfield, 1998
Black/White Relations in American History, by Leslie V. Tischauser,
　　1998
The Creation/Evolution Controversy, by James L. Hayward, 1998
The Beat Generation, by William Lawlor, 1998
Biographies of Scientists, by Roger Smith, 1998
Introducing Canada, by Brian Gobbett and Robert Irwin, 1998
*Four British Women Novelists: Anita Brookner, Margaret Drabble, Iris
　　Murdoch, Barbara Pym*, by George Soule, 1998
Thomas Hardy's Major Novels, by Julie Sherrick, 1998

Thomas Hardy's Major Novels

An Annotated Bibliography

Julie Sherrick

Magill Bibliographies

The Scarecrow Press, Inc.
Lanham, Md., & London
and
Salem Press
Pasadena, Calif., & Englewood Cliffs, N.J.
1998

SCARECROW PRESS, INC.

Published in the United States of America
by Scarecrow Press, Inc.
4720 Boston Way
Lanham, Maryland 20706

4 Pleydell Gardens, Folkestone
Kent CT20 2DN, England

British Library Cataloguing in Publication Information Available

Library of Congress Cataloging-in-Publication Data

Sherrick, Julie, 1963–
    Thomas Hardy's major novels : an annotated bibliography / Julie
Sherrick.
      p. cm. — (Magill bibliographies)
    ISBN 0-8108-3382-4 (alk. paper)
    1. Hardy, Thomas, 1840–1928—Fictional works—Bibliography.
I. Title. II. Series.
Z8386.5.S54   1998
[PR4757.F5]
016.823'8—dc21   98-3156
                                               CIP

To Randy, Alicia, and Allison

Table of Contents

Page

Acknowledgments xi

Foreword xiii

Chapter I - A Topical Guide to Subjects and Themes 1

Chapter II - Background Study on
Victorian England and Thomas Hardy 7

Chapter III - *Far from the Madding Crowd* 39
Circumstances of Composition 39
Comparative Studies 45
Nature of the Novel 49
Salient Features of the Novel 54
Character Analysis 57

Chapter IV - *The Return of the Native* 65
Circumstances of Composition 65
Comparative Studies 70
Nature of the Novel 72
Salient Features of the Novel 74
Character Analysis 78

Chapter V - *The Mayor of Casterbridge* 83
Circumstances of Composition 83
Comparative Studies 88
Nature of the Novel 91
Salient Features of the Novel 93
Character Analysis 97

Chapter VI - *The Woodlanders* 107
   Circumstances of Composition 107
   Comparative Studies 111
   Nature of the Novel 115
   Salient Features of the Novel 117
   Character Analysis 121

Chapter VII - *Tess of the d'Urbervilles* 123
   Circumstances of Composition 123
   Comparative Studies 131
   Nature of the Novel 137
   Salient Features of the Novel 141
   Character Analysis 145

Chapter VIII - *Jude the Obscure* 151
   Circumstances of Composition 151
   Comparative Studies 156
   Nature of the Novel 158
   Salient Features of the Novel 160
   Character Analysis 167

Appendix A
   Computer Connections 171

Appendix B
   Works Cited 173

About the Author 195

Acknowledgments

Even a small project of this kind requires the efforts of more than a single person. I would like to thank Theresa Shaffer for her help in obtaining the various articles and books through interlibrary loan services, and I would like to note that her work as a reference librarian is greatly appreciated by those who do research work at the Friedsam Memorial Library at St. Bonaventure University. I would also like to thank Dr. Anthony Farrow and Professor Philip Eberl for their help and encouragement throughout the original bibliography project as well as Dr. Lauren De La Vars, who has been both a friend and a mentor during much of the time that I have spent as a student and Adjunct Professor at St. Bonaventure University. Next, I would like to mention Alistair Chisholm of Dorset Safaris who provided Dr. De La Vars and myself with an excellent tour of Dorchester and the surrounding areas during the summer of 1997. Also, I wish to mention that I much appreciated the kindness of Andrew Leah, Secretary to the Thomas Hardy Society, upon my recent visit to Max Gate. I would like to extend a sincere *thank you* to project editor A. J. Sobczak for his help and advice regarding the successful completion of this volume. In addition, it should be noted that the comments offered by Dr. Jerry Long regarding the final draft version of the manuscript proved to be very helpful. Finally, I feel it is important to recognize the efforts of Diane Conklin, without whose computer knowledge and keyboarding skills this work would not have come together in its present form. Any errors noted in the following pages are, of course, my own.

Foreword

One interesting feature of Thomas Hardy's Dorchester house, Max Gate, is the shutter sash of solid planking that he could raise part way from its slot under his dining room window. Hardy designed this sash in order to screen his private life from peering sightseers out on the lawn without losing altogether the light from the sky above. Hardy's interest in windows must have stemmed from his childhood home, where the farm workers' pay-window was a feature of the ground floor office and his own bedroom window, tucked beneath the thatched eaves, looked towards the Admiral Hardy Monument high on a hill across the county. His architectural training and practice would have furthered his practical knowledge of windows, and his imagination led him to less technical interpretations.

As a permeable layer between the private and the public, windows were important to Hardy, in life and in fiction. In so many of Hardy's novels the views into and out of windows lead to pivotal events: Eustacia's glimpsing Mrs. Yeobright rapping at the cottage door in search of Clym; Susan and Elizabeth-Jane's spotting Michael Henchard presiding in the King's Arms banqueting hall; Sue Bridehead's leaping from the bedroom window to escape her husband Phillotson.

A century after his novels were published, readers and writers continue to broach new windows into Hardy's private life and his public writings. Hardy's Dorset homes and the supposed locations of his tales are regularly visited by the public he both courted and rebuffed. Hardy's fiction is enjoying a renaissance of popular and critical interest, with film and television adaptations spurring wider audiences to read and respond to *The Return of the Native* and *Jude the Obscure*. Recent critical trends have sparked extensive reevaluation of Hardy's characters, narrators, and historical and social contexts.

This scholarly and critical activity has yielded thousands of articles, books, notes, theses, and casebooks about Hardy. In 1928, the year of

Hardy's death, the Modern Language Association's annual bibliography listed four publications about Hardy. In 1995, that bibliography's list had grown to nearly fifty items related to Hardy. Sifting through this proliferation of scholarship and criticism is a daunting task for general readers and Hardy students.

The present volume, compiled by an English literature teacher of many years' experience, is an invaluable guide to the most helpful books and articles about Hardy's six most widely read novels. This bibliography is designed for general readers, secondary-level students and teachers, and college- and university-level students and teachers who require some direction in locating and assessing secondary criticism of Hardy's novels. Like Hardy's real and fictional windows, *Thomas Hardy's Major Novels: An Annotated Bibliography* frames and organizes a varied topography, in this case the principal accessible texts of modern Hardy scholarship and criticism.

Dr. Lauren Pringle De La Vars
Associate Professor of English
Saint Bonaventure University

A view of High Street in Dorchester.

Chapter I
A Topical Guide to Subjects and Themes

The following bibliography is an assembly of selected secondary sources that reflect trends in criticism within the last thirty years. The materials in the bibliography have been organized in such a way as to provide readers with access to information relating to various aspects of Hardy's six major novels. The materials that have been collected have been grouped into five distinct categories. Although some selections contain information that could perhaps place them within several subsections of a given chapter, in general, each work was placed within the category that was most clearly addressed by its overall premise or purpose. To those interested in discussions that address the major themes that run throughout the body of Hardy's works, the subsections titled "Salient Features" and "Character Analysis" are of special interest. (Chapter 2 provides annotations of large works that specifically address themes as well.)

Although a variety of themes have been identified and/or associated with Hardy's works, several major threads appear to run throughout the major fiction. Frequently addressed by critics is the theme of Time. In his article "Aspects of Time in *Far from the Madding Crowd*," Michael Goss discusses how Time, in both the universal and practical senses, affects the lives of the principal characters. Atkinson's article titled "The Inevitable Movement Onward—Some Aspects of *The Return of the Native*," discusses the sequence of events presented in the novel and argues that in Hardy's original conception of the novel, he did not attempt to create unity in terms of the timing of the incidents described. Time or timing is also viewed as being a significant feature in *The Mayor of Casterbridge*. Fussell explains how the lives of Michael Henchard, Susan, Lucetta, Elizabeth-Jane, and Donald Farfrae are influenced by the timing of particular events as well as the changing nature of the society in which they live. In addition, articles by Jane Adamson, Janet Freeman, Frank Giordano, and Forest Pyle address the importance of time in either the novel *Tess of the d'Urbervilles* or the novel *Jude the Obscure.*

Another important theme frequently addressed by critics is that of sight. E. M. Nollen discusses how the various perceptions of the characters Gabriel Oak, Farmer Boldwood, and Frank Troy (*Far from the Madding Crowd*) shape their actions as well as their respective relationships with Bathsheba Everdene. Other articles of interest relating to *Far from the Madding Crowd* are Peter Casagrande's "A New View of Bathsheba Everdene" and Judith Bryant Wittenberg's "Angles of Vision and Questions of Gender in *Far from the Madding Crowd.*" Lennart A. Bjork's article titled "Visible Essences as Thematic Structure in Hardy's *Return of the Native*" provides readers with insight into the influence of perceptions upon Clym Yeobright and Eustacia Vye. "Vision and Viewpoint in *The Mayor of Casterbridge*" by Robert Kiely focuses on Elizabeth-Jane's unique position as the observer within the novel. Finally, in "Ways of Looking at Tess," by Janet Freeman, Freeman describes how characters like Angel Clare and Alec d'Urberville fail to understand Tess because they are unable to truly recognize who she is.

The theme of the importance of education is perhaps most clearly seen in the novel *Jude the Obscure* (as noted in Patricia Alden's article relating to the genesis of this particular novel). However, the article by Simon Trezise titled "Ways of Learning in *The Return of the Native*" is also an interesting and informative study relating to the theme of education and/or the influence of learning. Finally, the article "Writing and Memory in *The Mayor of Casterbridge*" by Earl Ingersoll reveals the significance of learning relating to the development of Michael Henchard. Discussions of the theme of education also appear in various articles addressing Grace Melbury's growth as an individual in *The Woodlanders.*

The importance of the love/marriage relationship is addressed in a number of articles that focus on several of the major novels beginning with Lionel Adey's article titled "Styles of Love in *Far from the Madding Crowd*," continuing with J. T. McCullen's "Henchard's Sale of Susan in *The Mayor of Casterbridge*," and concluding with Frank Giordano's "Secularization and Ethical Authority in *Jude the Obscure.*"

The themes of heredity and/or the importance of family have been noted by numerous critics as well. In Anne Z. Mickelson's "The Family

Trap in *The Return of the Native*," she describes the significance of the relationship between Clym Yeobright and his mother. In "The Lure of Pedigree in *Tess of the d'Urbervilles*," William Greenslade identifies and describes Tess's and Angel's views on the importance of heredity, and in Cushla Beckingham's "The Importance of Family in Hardy's Fictional World," Beckingham includes information on the significance of heredity in Hardy's novels as well as his poems. In addition, in several studies relating to the nature of the novel *Jude the Obscure*, Jude's beliefs about the influence of his family's past upon his own life are discussed.

Finally, there are a number of full-length studies that specifically address the themes present in the body of Hardy's major fiction. Examples of such works are J. Hillis Miller's *Thomas Hardy: Distance and Desire*, Marjorie Garson's *Hardy's Fables of Integrity*, Virginia Hyman's *Ethical Perspective in the Novels of Thomas Hardy*, Ian Gregor's *The Great Web*, and Joseph Warren Beach's *The Technique of Thomas Hardy*. Also, it should be noted that two works by Michael Millgate, *Thomas Hardy: His Career as a Novelist* and *Thomas Hardy: A Biography*, provide readers with excellent information relating to a variety of aspects of Hardy's works. In the chapters directed to discussions of particular works, evidence focusing on the presence of particular themes within the various novels is often discussed.

Works Cited

Adamson, Jane. "Tess, Time, and Its Shapings." *The Critical Review* 26 (1984): 18-36.

Adey, Lionel. "Styles of Love in *Far from the Madding Crowd*." *Thomas Hardy Annual* 5 (1987): 47-62.

Alden, Patricia. "A Short Story Prelude to *Jude the Obscure*: More Light on the Genesis of Hardy's Last Novel." *The Colby Library Quarterly* 19.1 (1983): 45-52.

Atkinson, F. G. "The Invisible Movement Onward—Some Aspects of *The Return of the Native*." *The Thomas Hardy Yearbook* 3 (1972): 10-17.

Beach, Joseph Warren. *The Technique of Thomas Hardy.* New York: Russell and Russell, 1962.

Beckingham, Cushla R. "The Importance of Family in Hardy's Fictional World." *The Thomas Hardy Journal* 5.2 (1985): 62-68.

Bjork, Lennart A. " 'Visible Essences' as Thematic Structure in Hardy's *The Return of the Native.*" *English Studies* 53 (1972): 52-63.

Casagrande, Peter J. "A New View of Bathsheba Everdene." *Critical Approaches to the Novels of Thomas Hardy.* Ed. Dale Kramer. London: Macmillan, 1979. 50-73.

Freeman, Janet. "Highways and Cornfields: Space and Time in the Narration of *Jude the Obscure.*" *Colby Quarterly* 27.3 (1991): 161-173.

— — —. "Ways of Looking at Tess." *Studies in Philology* 79.3 (1982): 311-323.

Fussell, D. H. "The Maladroit Delay: The Changing Times in Hardy's *The Mayor of Casterbridge.*" *Critical Quarterly* 21.3 (1979): 17-29.

Garson, Marjorie. *Hardy's Fables of Integrity.* Oxford: Clarendon, 1991.

Giordano, Frank R. "Secularization and Ethical Authority in *Jude the Obscure.*" *The Thomas Hardy Yearbook* 3 (1972-1973): 34-40.

Goss, Michael. "Aspects of Time in *Far from the Madding Crowd.*" *The Thomas Hardy Journal* 6.3 (1990): 43-53.

Greenslade, William. "The Lure of Pedigree in *Tess of the d'Urbervilles.*" *The Thomas Hardy Journal* 7.3 (1991): 103-115.

Gregor, Ian. *The Great Web: The Form of Hardy's Major Fiction.* Totowa, New Jersey: Rowman and Littlefield, 1974.

Hyman, Virginia R. *Ethical Perspective in the Novels of Thomas Hardy.* New York: Kennikat Press, 1975.

Ingersoll, Earl G. "Writing and Memory in *The Mayor of Casterbridge*." *English Literature in Transition* 33.3 (1990): 299-309.

Kiely, Robert. "Vision and Viewpoint in *The Mayor of Casterbridge*." *Nineteenth-Century Fiction* 23.2 (1968): 189-200.

McCullen, J. T., Jr. "Henchard's Sale of Susan in *The Mayor of Casterbridge*." *English Language Notes* 2.3 (1965): 217-218.

Mickelson, Anne Z. "The Family Trap in *The Return of the Native*." *Colby Library Quarterly* 10.8 (1974): 463-475.

Miller, J. Hillis. *Thomas Hardy: Distance and Desire*. Cambridge: Harvard University Press, 1970.

Millgate, Michael. *Thomas Hardy: A Biography*. New York: Random House, 1982.

— — —. *Thomas Hardy: His Career as a Novelist*. New York: St. Martin's Press, 1994.

Nollen, E. M. "The Loving Look in *Far from the Madding Crowd*." *The Thomas Hardy Yearbook* 13 (1986): 69-73.

Wittenburg, Judith Bryant. "Angles of Vision and Questions of Gender in *Far from the Madding Crowd*." *The Centennial Review* 30 (1986): 25-40.

The Thomas Hardy statue looking west across Colliton Street, Dorchester.

Chapter II
Background Study on
Victorian England and Thomas Hardy

Thomas Hardy was born on June 2, 1840 and died in 1928. At the beginning of Victoria's reign, at the time of Hardy's birth, an enormous amount of social change was underway. The spread of industrialization had contributed to a shift in the overall economic structure of the nation, as had scientific discovery and technological advancement. As a result, social institutions such as the educational system, the church, and the individual family unit were forced to adapt to the new conditions. Hardy grew up during this period of rapid change, and thus his works reflect not only some of his personal concerns but also the concerns of the society to which he belonged. In his 1973 study *Victorian People and Ideas*, Richard D. Altick describes the literature of the Victorian Period as "the record of a society seeking ways to adjust itself to conditions as revolutionary as any we face today" (73). In describing one of Hardy's major novels (*Tess*), James Gibson says that it

> is concerned with important questions of human behavior, and to read it is to be brought into contact with a sensitive and comprehensive mind brooding over issues that are part of all our lives. (39)

The same can certainly be said about the five other major novels written by Hardy. Both Altick's and Gibson's comments point out the timeless nature of Hardy's works as well as the contemporary significance of the ideas addressed in novels like *Far from the Madding Crowd*, *The Return of the Native*, *The Mayor of Casterbridge*, *The Woodlanders*, *Tess of the d'Urbervilles*, and *Jude the Obscure*. Today's readers can clearly identify with Hardy's concerns as they are expressed throughout his major fiction and throughout the lives of the characters Hardy took so much care in developing.

Although much has been written about Hardy's life and works, several sources have been widely recognized as being of primary importance to those who wish to learn more about his life and times. The work by Michael Millgate titled *Thomas Hardy: A Biography* is generally considered to be the definitive work on Hardy. An earlier biography by Robert Gittings has also been recognized for its contribution to Hardy scholarship, and a new biography by Martin Seymour-Smith has been recently published by St. Martin's Press. Other interesting and helpful sources are the works of Timothy Hands, Jan Jedrzejewski, and Robert Langbaum. Even though Hands (1989) and Jedrzejewski (1996) both address similar topics involving Hardy's religious attitudes and beliefs, both works (*Thomas Hardy: Distracted Preacher* and *Thomas Hardy and the Church*) provide readers with a wealth of information. Langbaum's work *Thomas Hardy in Our Time* makes an important contribution to Hardy scholarship because he explains not only the appeal of Hardy's works but also their significance for the modern reader. In addition, it should be noted that while many works about Hardy include chronologies of his life, the chronology included in F. B. Pinion's *A Thomas Hardy Dictionary: With Maps and a Chronology* is of great use to readers, as is Timothy Hands's *A Hardy Chronology*. Also, it is important to note the work of Florence Hardy (believed to be largely autobiographical), as well as the various collections of Hardy's personal writings as compiled and edited by Harold Orel and Richard Taylor. Finally, for those interested in precise information concerning the composition and publication process relating to each of Hardy's works, R. L. Purdy's *Thomas Hardy: A Bibliographical Study* is invaluable.

Just as certain sources prove to be of special value to those interested in background information about Hardy, it should be pointed out that a variety of works are especially helpful to those wishing to gain insight regarding one or more of the major novels. For those studying particular aspects of *Far from the Madding Crowd*, the contributions of Robert C. Schweik should not go unnoticed. The works of J. Hillis Miller and Simon Trezise are particularly useful to students of *The Return of the Native*. In terms of *The Mayor of Casterbridge*, the work of Christine Winfield adds much to the study of the novel as does that of Ronald P. Draper and D. H. Fussell. Dale Kramer's and F. B. Pinion's articles provide excellent information regarding specific features of *The Woodlanders*, and for students of *Tess of the d'Urbervilles*, the works of Casagrande, Laird, and Pettit are of special interest. For information relating to distinguishing features of *Jude the Obscure*, the works of Patricia Ingham and Patricia Alden are of great value.

For those interested in more comprehensive studies of the major novels, there are a number of larger works that treat them as a whole and which should be recognized as significant additions to the body of literature written about Hardy and his major works. The following volumes are often identified, discussed, and cited within the criticism of recent years. They are:

Beach, Joseph Warren. *The Technique of Thomas Hardy*
Boumelha, Penny. *Thomas Hardy and Women: Sexual Ideology and Narrative Form*
Chase, Mary Ellen. *Thomas Hardy: From Serial to Novel*
Draper, Ronald P., and Phillip V. Mallett, eds. *A Spacious Vision: Essays on Hardy*
Fisher, Joe. *The Hidden Hardy*
Garsen, Marjorie. *Hardy's Fables of Integrity*
Gatrell, Simon. *Thomas Hardy and the Proper Study of Mankind*
Grimsditch, Herbert B. *Character and Environment in the Novels of Hardy*
Higonnet, Margaret, ed. *The Sense of Sex: Feminist Perspectives on Hardy*
Hyman, Virginia. *Ethical Perspective in the Novels of Thomas Hardy*
Jagdish, Chandra Dave. *The Human Predicament in Hardy's Novels*
Langbaum, Robert. *Thomas Hardy in Our Time*
Meisel, Perry. *The Return of the Repressed*
Miller, J. Hillis. *Thomas Hardy: Distance and Desire*
Millgate, Michael. *Thomas Hardy: His Career as a Novelist*
Rutland, William. *Thomas Hardy: A Study of His Writings and Their Background*
Taylor, Dennis. *Hardy's Literary Language and Victorian Philology*

Also, the work of Simon Gatrell should be recognized since his contributions as General Editor for The World Classics edition (published by Oxford University Press) prove of great value to current readers of Hardy's fiction. The care he has taken to ensure the authenticity of each text and the selection of various editors for individual editions of the major novels assure students and scholars that their own readings of the text(s) will be based on accurate information and careful documentation.

Readers of Hardy's major fiction should be aware that the body of information written about Hardy and his works is large and varied. The purpose of this present volume is to provide general readers with a collection of works with which they may further their own study of a particular novel or several of the novels. Although it is not comprehensive in scope, the bibliography includes annotations for approximately two hundred sources written over the course of a thirty- to forty-year period. Information relating to current software or information available on the Internet is included in Appendix A, and a complete listing of the works cited can be found in Appendix B. Lastly, for the ongoing discussion of Hardy's works, readers should consult current editions of *The Thomas Hardy Journal* published by The Thomas Hardy Society.

Works Cited

Alden, Patricia. "A Short Story Prelude to *Jude the Obscure*: More Light on the Genesis of Hardy's Last Novel." *The Colby Library Quarterly* 19.1 (1983): 45-52.

Altick, Richard. *Victorian People and Ideas*. New York: W. W. Norton & Company, 1973.

Beach, Joseph Warren. *The Technique of Thomas Hardy*. New York: Russell and Russell, 1962.

Boumelha, Penny. *Thomas Hardy and Women: Sexual Ideology and Narrative Form*. Sussex: Harvester Press, 1982.

Casagrande, Peter J. *"Tess of the d'Urbervilles": Unorthodox Beauty*. New York: Twayne, 1992.

Chase, Mary Ellen. *Thomas Hardy from Serial to Novel*. New York: Russell & Russell, 1964.

Draper, Ronald P. "*The Mayor of Casterbridge*." *Critical Quarterly* 25.1 (1983): 57-70.

— — —, and Phillip V. Mallett, eds. *A Spacious Vision: Essays on Hardy*. Newmill: Patten Press, 1994.

Fisher, Joe. *The Hidden Hardy*. New York: St. Martin's Press, 1992.

Fussell, D. H. "The Maladroit Delay: The Changing Times in Hardy's *The Mayor of Casterbridge*." *Critical Quarterly* 21.3 (1979): 17-29.

Garson, Marjorie. *Hardy's Fables of Integrity*. Oxford: Clarendon, 1991.

Gatrell, Simon. *Thomas Hardy and the Proper Study of Mankind*. Charlottesville: University Press of Virginia, 1993.

Gibson, James. "*Tess of the d'Urbervilles*." *The Thomas Hardy Journal* 7.3 (1991): 34-47.

Gittings, Robert. *Young Thomas Hardy: Thomas Hardy's Later Years*. New York: Quality Paperback Book Club, 1990.

Grimsditch, Herbert B. *Character and Environment in the Novels of Thomas Hardy*. New York: Russell and Russell, 1925 (Reissued 1962).

Hands, Timothy. *A Hardy Chronology*. London: Macmillan, 1992.

— — —. *Thomas Hardy: Distracted Preacher*. New York: St. Martin's Press, 1989.

Higonnet, Margaret R., ed. *The Sense of Sex: Feminist Perspectives on Hardy*. Chicago: University of Illinois Press, 1993.

Hyman, Virginia R. *Ethical Perspective in the Novels of Thomas Hardy*. New York: Kennikat Press, 1975.

Ingham, Patricia. "The Evolution of *Jude the Obscure*." *The Review of English Studies* 27 (1976): 27-37, 159-169.

Jagdish, Chandra Dave. *The Human Predicament in Hardy's Novels*. London: Macmillan, 1985.

Jedrzejewski, Jan. *Thomas Hardy and the Church*. New York: St. Martin's Press, 1996.

Kramer, Dale. "Two 'New' Texts of Thomas Hardy's *The Woodlanders*." *Studies in Bibliography* 20 (1967): 135-150.

Laird, John T. *The Shaping of "Tess of the d'Urbervilles."* London: Oxford University Press, 1975.

Langbaum, Robert. *Thomas Hardy in Our Time*. New York: St. Martin's Press, 1995.

Meisel, Perry. *Thomas Hardy: The Return of the Repressed*. New Haven, CT: Yale University Press, 1972.

Miller, J. Hillis. *Thomas Hardy: Distance and Desire*. Cambridge: Harvard University Press, 1970.

— — —. "Topography in *The Return of the Native*." *Essays in Literature* 8.2 (1981): 119-134.

Millgate, Michael. *Thomas Hardy: A Biography*. New York: Random House, 1982.

— — —. *Thomas Hardy: His Career as a Novelist*. New York: St. Martin's Press, 1994.

Orel, Harold, ed. *Thomas Hardy's Personal Writings*. Lawrence: University of Kansas Press, 1966.

Pettit, Charles P. C. "Hardy's Concept of Purity in *Tess of the d'Urbervilles*." *The Thomas Hardy Journal* 7.3 (1991): 48-57.

— — —. "Hardy's Vision of the Individual in *Tess of the d'Urbervilles*." *New Perspectives on Thomas Hardy*. Ed. Charles P. C. Pettit. New York: St. Martin's Press, 1994. 172-190.

Pinion, F. B. "The Country and Period of *The Woodlanders.*" *The Thomas Hardy Yearbook* 2 (1971): 46-55.

— — —. *A Thomas Hardy Dictionary.* New York: New York University Press, 1989.

Purdy, Richard L. *Thomas Hardy: A Bibliographical Study.* Oxford: Clarendon Press, 1968.

Rutland, William R. *Thomas Hardy: A Study of His Writings and Their Background.* New York: Russell & Russell, 1962.

Schweik, Robert C. "The Early Development of Hardy's *Far From the Madding Crowd.*" *Texas Studies in Literature and Language* 9 (1967): 414-428.

— — —. "An Error in the Text of Hardy's *Far from the Madding Crowd.*" *Colby Library Quarterly* VII.6 (1966): 269.

— — —. "A First Draft Chapter of Hardy's *Far from the Madding Crowd.*" *English Studies* 53 (1972): 344-349.

— — —. "The Narrative Structure of *Far from the Madding Crowd.*" *Budmouth Essays on Thomas Hardy.* Ed. F. B. Pinion. Dorchester: The Thomas Hardy Society, 1976. 21-38.

Seymour-Smith, Martin. *Hardy: A Biography.* New York: St. Martin's Press, 1994.

Taylor, Dennis. *Hardy's Literary Language and Victorian Philology.* Oxford: Clarendon Press, 1993.

Trezise, Simon. "Ways of Learning in *The Return of the Native.*" *The Thomas Hardy Journal* 7.2 (1991): 56-65.

Winfield, Christine. "The Manuscript of Hardy's *Mayor of Casterbridge.*" *The Papers of the Bibliographical Society of America* 67 (1973): 33-58.

Wright, Reg., ed. *Two English Masters: Charles Dickens and Thomas Hardy*. New York: Marshall Cavendish, 1989.

Barber, D. F., ed. *Concerning Thomas Hardy*. London: Charles Skilton, 1968.

Barber's approach to the biography is unique because "The genesis of this particular book dates back to 1958 when Mr. Stevens Cox conceived the idea of seeking out those people still alive who had known Hardy and asking them to write down their memories and reminiscences of the author" (xii-xiii). Barber explains that due to the nature of the information contained in the book, there are some contradictions within its text. Nevertheless, this approach is successful in its presentation of Hardy as a prolific author and a complicated man. Some points of special interest are the personal photographs and previously unpublished letters written by Hardy.

Beningfield, Gordon, and Anthea Zeman. *Hardy Country*. London: Allen Lane, 1983.

This book is filled with numerous illustrations by Gordon Beningfield with the text, excluding captions, having been prepared by Anthea Zeman. The paintings and sketches shown are beautifully done. The subject matter for each painting is some particular aspect or feature described by Hardy in one of his novels, short stories, or poems. The captions identify the location of the scene and wildlife being depicted. The narrative that runs throughout provides readers with more information about the settings described in Hardy's works, and specific examples from a variety of Hardy's works are given so that readers who are not familiar with the setting of a particular novel can appreciate the painting or sketch in question. Overall, the work enhances the reader's understanding and appreciation of Hardy's *Wessex*.

Boumelha, Penny. *Thomas Hardy and Women: Sexual Ideology and Narrative Form*. Sussex: Harvester Press, 1982.

Boumelha begins with a general discussion of sexual ideology as it existed and was expressed during much of the Victorian Period. She follows this with a chapter describing the novels written between the years 1871 and 1886. Boumelha also treats several of the novels individually, beginning with a discussion of *The Return of the Native*. She argues that "*The Return of the Native* most valuably prefigures the last novels" (61). Later chapters deal with newer trends in fiction as they relate to the critical interpretation of *Tess of the d'Urbervilles* and *Jude the Obscure*. She states:

> The formal characteristics of *Tess of the d'Urbervilles*, its increasingly overt confrontation of subjectivity and subjection, will enable the radical break in the relation of female character to narrative voice . . . (132)

Throughout her work, Boumelha focuses on the roles of female characters and refers to early as well as current feminist criticism.

Brasnett, Hugh. *Thomas Hardy: A Pictorial Guide.* Ringwood, Hampshire: Lodge Copse Press, 1990.
This black and white photo guide includes area maps that accompany many of the photographs, illustrating areas believed to be the originals for the settings described in Hardy's fiction. Of particular interest to those wishing to visit Dorset are the brief descriptions of various buildings and topographical features of the region. A good bit of historical information is provided for readers as well.

Bullen, J. B. *The Expressive Eye: Fiction and Perception in the Work of Thomas Hardy.* Oxford: Clarendon Press, 1986.
Bullen discusses this unique volume as an attempt

> to show how Hardy drew on his temperamental predisposition to structure his novels as a series of images, and to demonstrate something of the reciprocal relations between the conscious and unconscious Hardy within the fiction. (12)

He begins his discussion with a chapter titled "Hardy and the Visual Arts." Here, Bullen examines Hardy's beliefs about what constitutes Art and how Hardy may have been influenced by the writings of Ruskin as well as the ongoing "debate in the French press between the advocates of realism and symbolism on art . . ." (13). Later chapters are devoted to the discussion of the artistic aspects present in particular works, such as *Far from the Madding Crowd, The Mayor of Casterbridge,* and *Tess of the d'Urbervilles.* The titles of each of the chapters indicate the focus of Bullen's discussion in regard to a particular work. Also interspersed throughout Bullen's work are a variety of photographs of some of Hardy's own artwork, in addition to artwork that may have influenced Hardy's writing. Since Hardy often alludes to particular paintings or styles of art in his novels, the illustrations prove to be very helpful to an understanding of Bullen's assertions. The information presented by Bullen is useful and informative. The work is organized logically, and although parts of his discussion are somewhat complicated in nature, a careful study aids readers in their understanding of Hardy's major fiction.

Cox, R. G., ed. *Thomas Hardy: The Critical Heritage*. New York: Barnes & Noble, 1970.

The purpose of this edition is to "give a representative selection of the main documents illustrating the impact of [Hardy's] work upon contemporaries" (xiii). Cox organizes this large body of information chronologically on the basis of dates of initial publication. The section devoted to *Tess* includes thirteen reviews which appeared throughout 1891 and 1892. In general, the reviews are not positive. Hardy's contemporaries find problems with his form, style and content. Nevertheless, there are some positive notes within each review. One reviewer laments that "it is a singular commentary upon the open chances of English fiction that the strongest English novel of many years should have to be lopped into pieces and adapted through different periodicals before it succeeded in finding a complete hearing" (182). The reviews printed here offer unique insights regarding the reactions of the audience to what Hardy was writing and are helpful in generating discussion about the novel.

Draper, Ronald P., and Phillip V. Mallett, eds. *A Spacious Vision: Essays on Hardy*. Newmill: The Patten Press, 1994.

This collection of fourteen essays by a variety of Hardy scholars provides readers with an excellent sampling of current Hardy criticism. Of special interest to readers of any one or all of Hardy's six major novels are the essays by Dale Kramer ("Hardy's Style of the Moment"), Phillip Mallett ("Thomas Hardy: An Idiosyncratic Mode of Regard"), Robert Schweik ("The 'Modernity' of Hardy's *Jude the Obscure*"), and Rosemary Sumner (" 'The Adventure of the Unknown': Hardy, Lawrence and Development in the Novel"). In addition, Rosemarie Morgan's essay "Mothering the Text: Hardy's Vanishing Maternal Abode" provides readers with interesting insights regarding *The Return of the Native* in particular. Finally, it is important to note that several essays devoted to discussions of Hardy's poetry are also included in this selection.

Edwards, Anne-Marie. *In the Steps of Thomas Hardy*. Newbury, Berkshire: Countryside Books, 1989.

The organization of this book is primarily chronological as it guides its readers through the areas where Hardy lived and worked. Physical descriptions of the various settings described in the major novels are presented in order of the publication of the novels. Photographs and maps are provided. Although this work functions primarily as a travel guide for visitors to the Dorset area, it contains an abundance of information for readers who wish to gain insights regarding the landscapes of Hardy's fiction.

Gatrell, Simon. *Hardy the Creator: A Textual Biography*. Oxford: Clarendon Press, 1988.

Gatrell states that the purpose of his book is

> to combine an outline of Hardy's career as a writer of fiction—his dealings with editors, publishers, and printers in England and America—with further investigations into his creative activity at the successive stages of the development of his fiction. . . . (ix)

The information is, in general, organized chronologically, and particular attention is paid to the details surrounding the publication history of each of the major novels. In chapter 11, titled "Editing Hardy," Gatrell discusses Hardy's use of punctuation and the rules that govern the current trends in the editing of Hardy's texts. He follows this chapter with a brief overview of the conclusions that can be drawn from researching the development of Hardy's fiction. Gatrell also includes an appendix that contains an extensive chronology and a table illustrating the number of *Hardy's Works as Published by Macmillan 1895-1939*. This volume is extremely helpful and informative to both the general and scholarly reader.

Gatrell, Simon. *Thomas Hardy and the Proper Study of Mankind*. Charlottesville: University Press of Virginia, 1993.

Although Gatrell does devote some discussion to several of the minor novels as well as specific selections of Hardy's poetry, what seems to bring this work together are his comments regarding the distinguishing features of the major novels. The chapters devoted to individual discussions of *The Return of the Native* (chapter 3), *The Mayor of Casterbridge* (chapter 5), *Tess of the d'Urbervilles* (chapter 6), and *Jude the Obscure* (chapter 8) are informative as well as interesting. In addition, although Gatrell identifies specific aspects of each novel on an individual basis, he also draws connections between and among the various works. For example, in the chapter titled *"The Mayor of Casterbridge*: The Fate of Michael Henchard's Character," Gatrell observes that, "In some interesting ways *The Mayor of Casterbridge* can be seen as a sequel to *The Return of the Native*" (70). Concerning two of Hardy's later novels, Gatrell states, "Hardy had already charted in *Tess of the d'Urbervilles* the decline of traditional rural community; in *Jude the Obscure* he traces the consequences for the individual of this decline" (155). Finally, Gatrell includes several chapters that complement his discussions of the individual works. One such chapter, titled "Angel Clare's Story" (also published separately in *The Thomas Hardy Journal*), relates Tess's story from Angel's point of view. This chapter, in conjunction with the others, serves to provide readers with a variety of fresh perspectives regarding Hardy's works.

Gerber, Helmut E., and W. Eugene Davis, eds. *Thomas Hardy: An Annotated Bibliography of Writings About Him*. DeKalb: Northern Illinois University Press, 1974.

The bibliography prepared by Gerber and Helmut demonstrates a thorough and comprehensive study of the works written about Thomas Hardy. The bibliography covers a period of 99 years and is organized chronologically, beginning with works published in the year 1871 and ending with works written in the year 1969. This 99-year period is broken down into four distinct periods which represent specific developments in Hardy's literary career and critical reputation (9). The scope of the work is clearly outlined in the preface, as are the criteria for inclusion in the bibliography. The bibliography is both comprehensive and carefully compiled. The abstracts are helpful and informative, and the format makes the work accessible.

Giordano, Frank R., Jr. *"I'd Have My Life Unbe"*: *Thomas Hardy's Self-Destructive Characters*. Tuscaloosa, Alabama: University of Alabama Press, 1984.

Giordano begins with a general review of the nature of critical discussion, early and late, of the novels. Next, he discusses the beliefs held by Victorians regarding suicide. Giordano states:

> From 1840 through 1938, which corresponds fairly closely to Hardy's life, the subject of human self-destructiveness challenged the minds and hearts

and stimulated the inquiries of physicians, historians, sociologists, psychoanalysts, and creative artists. (23)

Later, Giordano identifies and describes the list of characters in the six major novels whose self-destructive tendencies end in death. Subsequent chapters address, and are titled after, the circumstances of the individual characters. Giordano describes the deaths of Eustacia Vye and Michael Henchard as Egoist suicides, the deaths of Farmer Boldwood and Jude the Obscure as Anomic suicides, and the deaths of Giles Winterborne and Tess Durbeyfield as Altruistic suicides. In the final chapter of his book, Giordano restates his observation that Hardy had a "long-evolving sensitivity to modern man's declining zest for life" (182), and that this sensitivity is reflected throughout his works.

Gittings, Robert. *Young Thomas Hardy* and *Thomas Hardy's Later Years*. New York: Quality Paperback Book Club, 1990.

This edition includes both previously published works by Robert Gittings in a single volume. Prior to the work by Michael Millgate (*Thomas Hardy: A Biography*), the two volumes, titled *Young Thomas Hardy* and *Thomas Hardy's Later Years*, were generally accepted as providing readers with the best biographical information about Hardy. Although some of Gittings' views have since been challenged, the biography as it exists in single volume form still merits examination. The material presented by Gittings is organized in a logical fashion and the writing is pleasant to read. Interspersed throughout the text are a number of photographs, and Gittings' personal observations are interesting and thought provoking.

Green, Brian. *Hardy's Lyrics: Pearls of Pity*. New York: St. Martin's Press, 1996.

Although Green's central purpose is to articulate what he feels is the unifying theme in Hardy's lyrics, he points out that his

definition of Hardy's master theme colligates various isolated, but logically linked, instances of a chain of concern that persists throughout those writings—his notebooks, letters, autobiography, essays, prefaces, novels and short stories—but mainly the novels. (3)

Therefore, Part I (titled "Hardy's Master Theme") of Green's book is of special interest to students of the novels. In this opening section, Green discusses the early critical reception of Hardy's novels. He also describes the views of more contemporary critics as well as Hardy's own views regarding the nature of his fiction. Green suggests the adoption of the term "cosmic process" to encompass Hardy's concerns regarding the "material conditions of man's life" (30). He also describes Hardy's concerns about human suffering as brought about through various circumstances. Later, Green turns to a discussion of the poetry. He provides numerous examples to support his assertion of a centralizing theme, and although his discussions are somewhat complicated, his writing is clear and precise. In general, his study is interesting and provides rewards for the reader.

Gregor, Ian. *The Great Web: The Form of Hardy's Major Fiction.* Totowa, New Jersey: Rowman and Littlefield, 1974.

In this full-length discussion, Gregor essentially examines the connections between and among Hardy's six major novels. Gregor says:

> Hardy's kind of fiction dramatizes a third-person consciousness, in which experiences, and reflection upon experience, become an integral part of his imaginative act. (31)

Throughout chapter 1, titled "Reading Hardy," Gregor discusses the criticism of Henry James and compares the form of Hardy's writing to the form described in his criticism and illustrated by James in his own writing of fiction. Later in the chapter, Gregor uses a remark made by Hardy to establish the idea that when read in conjunction with each other, Hardy's six major novels create a web-like pattern. This pattern, asserts Gregor, reveals "an overall movement in the interrelationship between the novels" (33). After establishing the premise of his arguments in the opening chapter, Gregor devotes a full chapter to individual discussions of each of the major novels. The titles of the chapters are as follows: "The Creation of Wessex: *Far from the Madding Crowd*," "Landscape with Figures: *The Return of the Native*," "A Man and His History: *The Mayor of Casterbridge*," "The Great Web: *The Woodlanders*," " 'Poor Wounded Name': *Tess of the D'Urbervilles*," and "An End and a Beginning: *Jude the Obscure.*" Gregor's approach to the major fiction is unique, and his observations are intriguing. The information contained in this volume is presented in a logical and organized manner, and other critics of Hardy's fiction often cite this particular work by Gregor within their own discussions of Hardy's novels.

Hands, Timothy. *A Hardy Chronology*. London: Macmillan, 1992.

This helpful volume provides readers with an abundance of easily accessible information relating to numerous significant events in Hardy's life. Hands relies on standard and well-documented sources for his information and organizes the material in a way that permits readers to locate information at a glance. The chronology covers Hardy's entire life span, and the individual months and years under discussion are marked in boldface type. Some historical information is provided but is specifically limited due to the scope of the chronology.

Hands, Timothy. *Thomas Hardy*. New York: St. Martin's Press, 1995.

Hands's work explores the development of Hardy's ideas as they are reflected in his writings by thoroughly examining Hardy's life in relationship to the time period in which he lived. Although, as stated by Hands, the longevity of Hardy's life renders this a complicated and difficult task, it is essential to a more complete understanding of the Hardy canon. Chapter 2 is especially interesting because Hands describes the influence of the Romantics upon Hardy. He distinguishes between the point of view of the Romantics and that of the Victorians. Hands also includes the full text of a variety of poems by Hardy and looks at them in relationship to the poetry of the Romantic period. Chapter 3 is also of special interest as in it Hands discusses Hardy's interest in education as an agent of change. He states "Hardy's treatment of education reflects the texture of reform dominating his period" (65). Hands goes on to say:

> Hardy's novels commonly depend on a contrast between an under-educated community and a hero or heroine (or both) who are educated beyond that community's level. (67)

The final chapter is notable because of its unique approach in organizing the critical reception of Hardy's work. The critical works examined and evaluated by Hands are organized by topic rather than chronologically. Significant works are highlighted for the reader. Hands makes the observation that Hardy "is too multiform to be orderly placed" (186). Overall, Hands' study provides a wealth of helpful information and is organized in such a way as to make it accessible to a wide audience.

Hands, Timothy. *Thomas Hardy: Distracted Preacher*. New York: St. Martin's Press, 1989.

Hands' book is divided into five chapters. They are titled "Hardy's Religious Biography," "Hardy's Use of Biblical Allusion," "Hardy's Characters," "Hardy and Christian Doctrine," and "Hardy's Religious Art." In chapter 1 Hands outlines chronologically the development of Hardy's religious practices and beliefs. He discusses Hardy's church attendance and the relationship between Hardy's family and the local parish. In chapter 2, Hands explains how Hardy's association with the Evangelical Movement contributed to his use of scriptural allusion. In the next chapter, Hands identifies five types of religious characters that reappear in various forms throughout many of Hardy's novels. Here he devotes much discussion to *Tess of the d'Urbervilles* and *Jude the Obscure*. In the following chapter, Hands addresses the disagreement among scholars regarding Hardy's actual attitudes toward Christian doctrine. He states, "The complexity of Hardy's attitude to the Christian religion is the root cause of such disagreement" (80). The final chapter of Hands' book broadens the scope of his argument and looks at "the contribution of Hardy's religious impetus to his artistic achievement" (107). Overall, Hands's work is interesting and informative. He addresses difficult topics in an organized manner.

Hardy, Thomas. *The Life and Works of Thomas Hardy 1840-1928*. Ed. Michael Millgate. Athens: University of Georgia Press, 1985.

This important source brings together the two volumes titled *The Early Life of Thomas Hardy 1840-1891* (1928) and *The Later Years of Thomas Hardy 1892-1928* (1930), previously published under the name of Florence Hardy (Thomas Hardy's second wife). This particular edition is valuable because each of the volumes originally attributed to Florence has been widely consulted by Hardy scholars and enthusiasts, and there has been much debate regarding the extent of Hardy's personal contributions to each of the two volumes. To help readers better understand the nature of the controversy pertaining to the authorship of the autobiography/biography, Millgate has included a detailed and fairly lengthy introduction as well as a brief section that explains the editorial procedures that he employed when creating this single-volume edition. In referring to the previously published works, Millgate states:

> It would, of course, be feasible to regard the *Life* as a work of shared or at any rate successive authorship, the product of a collaboration between Thomas Hardy and Florence Emily Hardy. (xxx)

Millgate also provides readers with information about the original publication process and the editorial procedures that were used at the time of the initial printing of each of the two volumes. It is important to note that works edited or written by Michael Millgate are highly esteemed by both scholars and general readers. Millgate's writing is clear, and he presents material in an organized and logical manner.

"Hardy, Thomas." *The Oxford Companion to English Literature.* Ed. Margaret Drabble. New York: Oxford University Press, 1985.
This brief entry contains a short chronology of Hardy's life and works. Also discussed is "the underlying theme of many of the novels ... the struggle of man against the indifferent force that rules the world and inflicts on him the sufferings and worries of life and love" (433). In addition, original publication dates are given for the majority of Hardy's works. This source is useful for obtaining general information.

"Hardy, Thomas." *The Penguin Companion to English Literature.* Ed. David Daiches. New York: McGraw-Hill, 1971.
This selection provides a brief summary of the major events in Hardy's life and gives information about the publication of Hardy's major works. Short statements regarding the theme and content of the works are also included. This source is suitable for providing general background information on Hardy and his works.

Hawkins, Desmond. *Thomas Hardy: His Life and Landscape.* N. P.: The National Trust, 1990.
This small paperback book provides readers with a wealth of background information about Thomas Hardy's life and writings. Numerous color photographs are included throughout the text, and the overall presentation of the material is straightforward and accessible. Materials published by the National Trust are especially helpful for those who are unfamiliar with the Dorset area and who wish to learn about the nature of a particular area or region described in Hardy's novels or poems.

Jackson, Arlene M. *Illustration and the Novels of Thomas Hardy.* Totowa, New Jersey: Rowman and Littlefield, 1981.
Although Jackson provides interesting commentary on the various scenes depicted in the series of illustrations included in her book, the illustrations themselves are the outstanding feature in the work. The

illustrations selected by Jackson help give readers unique visual representations of a number of well-known scenes depicted through Hardy's language in the novels. The pictorial record of illustrations also gives readers insights regarding Victorian modes of dress and points of view. Jackson's discussions of the different plates relating to the specific novels aids in giving the reader a better understanding of the demands of serial publication. Also worth noting are the accounts of Hardy's reaction to a particular illustration and his relationship with the various illustrators themselves. Overall, the work is useful to readers because it provides them with a group of illustrations that would otherwise be relatively difficult to access.

Jedrzejewski, Jan. *Thomas Hardy and the Church.* New York: St. Martin's Press, 1996.

Jedrzejewski continues the study of Thomas Hardy's attitudes regarding Christianity, and while he recognizes the work of Timothy Hands (*Thomas Hardy: Distracted Preacher*) as an important and detailed work, he feels that it has failed in some aspects. Jedrzejewski argues that earlier studies, like Hands', often treat Hardy's beliefs as having been formed early in his life rather than throughout his life. As a result, he takes a more unique approach to his study of Hardy's opinions as reflected in "the church-related motifs and images—church architecture, church music, and the characters of clergymen" (6). Beginning with a chapter titled "Hardy's Religious Biography" (incidentally, the exact title Hands uses for the first chapter of his book), Jedrzejewski provides background information on religious upbringing as well as the prevailing ideologies of the time period. Subsequent chapters focus on an analysis of the three topics referred to above. Throughout his work, Jedrzejewski cites numerous examples from the texts of the novels and poems as well as from Hardy's personal notes. Of special interest is chapter 4, titled "Hardy's Clerical Characters." Here, Jedrzejewski examines the relationship between Hardy and Arthur George Sewallis Shirly, the Stinsford parish priest, as well as Hardy's various encounters with other clergymen including "the notorious case of the Bishop of Wakefield's burning of a copy of *Jude the Obscure*" (181). He goes on to explain how these relationships are reflected in the characters Hardy created. Jedrzejewski concludes his study by restating the necessity of not oversimplifying the complex nature of Hardy's beliefs.

Kramer, Dale, ed. *Critical Approaches to the Fiction of Thomas Hardy.* New York: Macmillan, 1979.

This collection of essays represents the views of a number of Hardy scholars relating to a variety of topics. However, the work is generally organized around discussions of the major fiction. The first three essays represent a more comprehensive approach to Hardy's fiction, while the remaining essays typically address a specific aspect of a particular novel. Individual essays on *Far from the Madding Crowd, The Mayor of Casterbridge, The Woodlanders, Tess of the d'Urbervilles,* and *Jude the Obscure* are included within the work.

Langbaum, Robert. *Thomas Hardy in Our Time.* New York: St. Martin's Press, 1995.

Langbaum has divided his book into five sections and addresses the material in such a way as to render it as useful to those who have read many of Hardy's novels as it is to those who have perhaps read only one. He begins with a section that compares the works of Hardy to the works of D. H. Lawrence. Langbaum points out that Lawrence readily acknowledged his debt to Hardy and feels that Lawrence's works move in a similar direction to Hardy's. The next chapter deals with an examination of Hardy's poetry. Langbaum analyzes opposing critical interpretations regarding the poetry and defends its appeal. He makes an interesting case in distinguishing between what he feels are minor or major poems. Langaum's discussion of the poems serves to set the groundwork for chapter 3, titled "Versions of the Pastoral." Langbaum argues that

> *The Return of the Native* is Hardy's greatest nature poem. Hardy achieves the imaginative freedom and intensity of great poetry by daring to make the heath the novel's central character . . . (64)

Chapter 4 focuses on aspects of works that make it possible to claim that they contain a "mixture of genres" (102). In the final chapter, titled "The Minimization of Sexuality," Langbaum devotes a great deal of discussion to the novels *The Mayor of Casterbridge* and *The Well-Beloved.* His arguments deal primarily with the lack of sexual feeling demonstrated by the principal characters in the respective novels. Overall, the book is well organized and the various topics are fully addressed.

Lefebure, Molly. *Thomas Hardy's World: The Life, Times and Works of the Great Novelist and Poet*. London: Carlton Books Limited, 1996.

This oversize volume records through color photographs and narrative some of the more well-known aspects of Hardy's life. Included are pictures of Hardy's childhood home as well as some of the other homes where Hardy lived during his career as a novelist and poet. Background information on Hardy's life is also provided, as are details surrounding the composition and publication of each of the major novels. Accompanying the discussions of the major works are selected photos of scenes recorded in the novels portrayed in several of the most recent film versions. The shots are easily recognized as stills from the film versions of the following: *Far from the Madding Crowd*, *The Return of the Native*, *The Mayor of Casterbridge*, *The Woodlanders*, *Tess of the d'Urbervilles*, and *Jude the Obscure*. Overall, this work provides readers with useful information, and it is organized in such a way as to render the information highly accessible. The photographs are beautiful and are placed throughout the volume. Not a page of the volume is to be missed by those who would wish for a glimpse of Hardy or his *Wessex*.

Lewis, C. Day, and R. A. Scott-James. *Thomas Hardy*. London: F. Mildner & Sons, 1965.

This small handbook is divided into three sections. Section I begins with a discussion of *Wessex* as a unique creation in fiction, followed by some brief biographical information about Hardy's early life. Also discussed are the various attributes of the major novels as compared to the deficiencies of the minor. The conclusion drawn by Scott-James at the end of this section is that "Hardy, a meditative poet, gave to the novel a sublimity to which in his own country it had not attained before" (28). In Section II, Scott-James describes *The Dynasts* as being an epic as well as a drama. He gives a description of Hardy's subject matter and provides analysis of individual stanzas. The final section, an essay by C. D. Lewis, focuses on criticism of Hardy's poetry. He comments that

> Personalities as a rule should be kept out of the criticism of poetry. But it is extraordinarily difficult, and possibly undesirable, to disassociate Hardy's poetry from his character. (36)

Lewis also notes that much of what is characteristic in Hardy's poetry does not change throughout the years. In other words, features that are found in the early poems are also found in those composed much later in Hardy's career. He goes on to comment on several popular poems, and concludes by praising Hardy's poetic achievement. This book provides a straightforward discussion of the more well-known aspects of Hardy and his work.

Millgate, Michael, ed. *Letters of Emma and Florence Hardy*. Oxford: Clarendon Press, 1996.

Michael Millgate's introduction to this volume of collected letters helps readers to better understand their significance. Millgate explains the nature of certain groups of correspondence as well as what may have happened to missing letters. What follows, presented in chronological order, are transcriptions of the letters of Emma Lavina Gifford, and then those of Florence Emily Dugdale, Hardy's first and second wives respectively. As with Millgate's other works, great attention has been paid to the smallest detail, and the material is presented in a logical and accessible format.

Millgate, Michael. *Thomas Hardy: A Biography*. New York: Random House, 1982.

The biography by Michael Millgate provides a thorough study of the life and works of Thomas Hardy. Included in this comprehensive work are discussions of each of Hardy's major novels; details relating to their composition, publication, and critical reception; and information regarding the influence of Hardy's life and philosophy upon these works. Detailed accounts of specific events in Hardy's life are also outlined, and the people and places he knew are carefully described. Numerous personal photographs are interspersed throughout the text. In addition, maps and outlines of the Hardy family tree are provided. The material contained in the biography is clearly and logically presented. It is recognized by numerous critics as the definitive source for information about Hardy as a man and as an author.

Orel, Harold. *The Final Years of Thomas Hardy, 1912-1928*. Lawrence: University Press of Kansas, 1976.

Orel focuses on the circumstances of Hardy's life late in his career when he had made the transition from novelist to poet. He devotes an entire chapter to a discussion of Hardy's relationship with his first wife, Emma. Orel also discusses Hardy's views on nature as well as his thoughts on Christianity. He includes numerous and various excerpts from Hardy's poetry throughout the text and explains how Hardy's views are reflected in his writings. In general, he approaches his subject from a unique perspective and his insights prove helpful to both the general and scholarly reader.

Orel, Harold, ed. *Thomas Hardy's Personal Writings*. Lawrence: University of Kansas Press, 1966.

This volume, edited by Harold Orel, provides readers with an extensive collection of Hardy's nonfiction/personal writings. The writings by Hardy are grouped into four major sections and are organized chronologically within each section. Section I includes the prefaces to Hardy's novels, and Section II includes the prefaces written by Hardy for the works of various other writers. Section III includes works that express Hardy's views on literary matters, and Section IV includes Hardy's writings involving personal reflections or reminiscences. Because Hardy often expressed his personal feelings about a particular novel in its preface, and since Hardy often responded to the comments of his critics within such pieces, a reading of the prefaces sheds much light on Hardy's views about writing. Also, Hardy's writings about literature are widely discussed throughout current criticism. Two essays by Hardy frequently mentioned by critics are included in Section III of Orel's book; they are "The Profitable Reading of Fiction" and "Candor in English Fiction." In general, this work provides readers with a group of materials that would be less accessible in their original form.

Orel, Harold. *The Unknown Thomas Hardy: Lesser-Known Aspects of Hardy's Life and Career*. Brighton, East Sussex: Harvester Press, 1987.

Orel's book appears to have been a springboard to a number of subsequent works by other scholars. He addresses in seven lengthy essays, marked by chapter headings, Hardy's career as an architect, his involvement in the theater, his friendships and his interest in the law, as well as the science of archeology. Orel also devotes an entire chapter to a discussion of *The Dynasts*, a work that he feels has been overlooked by numerous critics. Orel's work is pleasant to read and very informative. Chapter 3, titled "Literary Friendships," explores Hardy's relationship with Rudyard Kipling and Henry Rider Haggard. Orel points to Kipling's "A Conference of the Powers," a short story where the central character, Mr. Cleever, resembles Hardy in a variety of ways as being of special interest. The final chapter, "Hardy and the Developing Science of Archeology," helps shed light on Hardy's interest in the past as well as his many references to historical artifacts. In general, Orel's work achieves its goal to "clarify our sense of the kind of man Thomas Hardy was, and send us back, refreshed, to his fiction and to his poetry" (11).

Pettit, Charles P. C., ed. *Celebrating Thomas Hardy*. New York: St. Martin's Press, 1996.

This book provides readers with a collection of some of the principal lectures given by a group of widely recognized Hardy scholars (as well as several selections by those who describe themselves as Hardy enthusiasts). The lectures were given in Dorchester at the 11th International Thomas Hardy Conference. The topics covered range from discussions of Hardy's poetry or novels to discussions of Hardy's personal relationships with family members or special friends. Each of the recorded lectures is unique in its approach, but when read in conjunction with one another these lectures help readers to better understand the nature of Hardy's wide-ranging appeal. One lecture (essay) of special interest to the general reader is "The Far and the Near: On Reading Thomas Hardy Today" by Peter Rothermel. Here, he describes his reactions and the reactions of his students to several of Hardy's major novels. Rothermel is able to articulate the substance of the appeal of various novels as well as to point out aspects that provide difficulty for modern readers. Also of interest are the selections by Michael Millgate, James Gibson, and Rosemarie Morgan. In general, this collection provides readers with the opportunity to become exposed to the thoughts and particular interests of some of the leaders in current Hardy criticism.

Pinion, F. B. *A Hardy Companion: A Guide to the Works of Thomas Hardy and Their Background*. London: Macmillan, 1968.

Pinion's work includes a wide range of information useful to the student of Hardy's works. Included in the work are an extensive chronology of Hardy's life; a section devoted to a discussion of each of Hardy's novels, short stories, and poems; and several sections or chapters which explore Hardy's views on topics such as art, tragedy, Christianity, and politics. Also included in the text is a "Dictionary of People and Places in Hardy's Works" (225). The references to specific novels which occur throughout the text deal primarily with their relationship to other works by Hardy or with the circumstances of composition. The photographs and maps contained in the "companion" serve as points of reference for the reader who is not familiar with Hardy's background or with his creation of *Wessex*. The specific references to *Jude the Obscure* provide insights regarding Hardy's possible intention in writing the novel as well as its relationship to his other works.

Pinion, F. B. *Thomas Hardy: His Life and His Friends*. New York: St. Martin's Press, 1996.

Included in Pinion's unique study are several helpful maps and a series of photographs. The approach taken by Pinion serves to help readers better understand how Hardy was influenced by those with whom he associated. The information is presented chronologically and Pinion has taken care to keep well within the range of the factual. Of special interest are the chapters titled "The Moules of Fordington" and "Leslie Stephen." Chapter 5 focuses on the Moules in general and on Hardy's relationship to Horace Moule in particular. Also presented in this chapter is information about the advice given to Hardy by Moule regarding Hardy's educational and occupational choices and opportunities. Later, in the chapter describing Hardy's relationship to Leslie Stephen, Pinion provides information about Stephen's friendship with Hardy as well as their working relationship. Comments made by Stephen as editor of the *Cornhill* in response to Hardy's submissions to the magazine are noted, as is Stephen's overall reaction to publishing anything that might offend his reading audience. Chapters 16 (*Max Gate, The Woodlanders,* and *Italy*), 17 (*Tales* and *Tess*), and 18 (*Jude* and *Consequences*) provide readers with additional insights regarding the events that were taking place in Hardy's life while he was writing each of the novels. Pinion concludes his work by providing testimony of Hardy's greatness in the words of several of his friends. This work (as well as other works by Pinion) provides readers with a wealth of information. His writing is clear and the topics he chooses to discuss are thoroughly handled. His scholarship is recognized by Hardy critics and enthusiasts alike.

Pinion, F. B. *A Thomas Hardy Dictionary*. New York: New York University Press, 1989.

Included in this excellent reference tool is an extensive chronology of Hardy's life with references to the dates of composition and publication of Hardy's novels. Also included is a series of maps that illustrate the settings of several of the novels as well as those that show actual place names of existing or previously existing areas. The dictionary entries themselves include descriptions of fictional characters and settings, as well as descriptions of existing and historical people, places, and cultural artifacts. Literary allusions are identified as such, and definitions for antiquated expressions are provided.

Purdy, Richard L. *Thomas Hardy: A Bibliographical Study*. Oxford: Clarendon Press, 1968.

Purdy's bibliography provides a comprehensive record of Hardy's publications, but it also presents the information in such a way as to render it especially useful to students of Hardy. He describes each volume in detail and also includes notes filled with biographical, historical, and background information on the particular work being examined. Each of the major works for *Tess of the d'Urbervilles* clearly outline the chronological order of the various publications and discuss the nature and scope of Hardy's revisions of the text.

Saxelby, Outwin F. *A Thomas Hardy Dictionary*. 1911. New York: Humanities Press, 1962.

Saxelby's dictionary includes not only explanations of various terms and identifications for the numerous characters that appear in Hardy's works, but also a synopsis of each of the novels and several maps which represent the fictional *Wessex*. In addition, Saxelby gives some biographical information about Hardy and provides a list of the first editions of Hardy's works. The dictionary provides useful information; however, it is important to note that as it was first published in 1911 more complete information may be available in other sources.

Seymour-Smith, Martin. *Hardy: A Biography*. New York: St. Martin's Press, 1994.

This lengthy biography provides readers with a wealth of information regarding the life and works of Thomas Hardy. The nearly forty chapters are organized chronologically, and many of Hardy's novels are discussed in individual chapters bearing their names. Like the biographies prepared by Robert Gittings and Michael Millgate, this volume includes a variety of photographs and other illustrations. Seymour-Smith often challenges the views taken by other scholars and the tone of the work is markedly different from previously published biographies on Hardy.

Springer, Marlene. *Hardy's Use of Allusion.* Lawrence: University Press of Kansas, 1983.

Springer discusses many of Thomas Hardy's works. She begins with a discussion of Hardy's style in general and then focuses on specific works in subsequent chapters. After this brief introduction, Springer specifically outlines the types of allusion used by Hardy, and gives several examples of each type. Her examination of the texts is thorough and offers many insights regarding the significance of certain passages within the novels. She closes her arguments by re-emphasizing the importance of recognizing the various allusions used by Hardy. She says:

> Hardy drew from many worlds to enlarge his own novelistic universe, making his allusions serve his audience as avenues into his fiction . . . He requires of his readers that they bring to his novels an imaginative effort, that they read as connoisseurs. (174)

Sutherland, J. A. *Victorian Novelists and Publishers.* Chicago: University of Chicago Press, 1976.

This volume provides readers with access to pertinent information about novel publication during the Victorian period. In part I, Sutherland describes the practices of novelists and publishers as they evolved throughout the 19th century. Of special interest to readers of Hardy's works is chapter 10, titled "Hardy Breaking into Fiction." Here, Sutherland describes in some detail how Hardy began his negotiations with various publishers, editors, and critics. At the close of the chapter, Sutherland states:

> What one can say is that Hardy gained from his early contact with the trade a sure awareness of the rules and fashions which dominated English fiction; he came to know his enemy. (225)

Overall, Sutherland's work provides a great deal of helpful information throughout the volume, and the chapter on Hardy addresses a number of significant aspects relating to Hardy's early experiences as a writer of fiction.

Taylor, Dennis. *Hardy's Literary Language and Victorian Philology.* Oxford: Clarendon Press, 1993.

Taylor's book is an extensive and thorough study of Hardy's use of language, his relationship to the development of the *Oxford English Dictionary*, and its impact on current linguistic study. He says:

> The breadth of Hardy's vocabulary is deeply rooted in his experience of Victorian philology . . . He illustrates a new consciousness of the English language, with its complex classifications, its complex word choice to other languages and to its own past. (172)

Taylor spends a great deal of time exploring the types of notes taken by Hardy regarding literary style and language use. He examines both early and late sources on which Hardy depended for advice. He describes Hardy's early training in grammar as a schoolboy as well as his concentrated efforts, in later life, to learn how best to express his ideas. Much more could be said about Taylor's fascinating study, but as his discourse is complicated and filled with an astonishing amount of detail, it is best examined slowly and thoroughly.

Taylor, Richard H., ed. *The Personal Notebooks of Thomas Hardy.* New York: Columbia University Press, 1979.

Found in this unique volume are transcriptions of four of Hardy's personal notebooks. The notebooks included in this volume are titled "Memoranda I," "Memoranda II," "Schools of Painting Notebook," and "Trumpet-Major Notebook." Taylor also provides detailed physical descriptions of each notebook as well as information relating to the principles he employed in the process of transcription. The work is useful to scholars as well as the diligent general reader. Taylor has taken great care to present the information in an accurate and accessible manner.

Temple, Ruth Z., and Martin Tuclar, eds. *A Library of Literary Criticism: Modern British Literature.* Volume II. New York: Frederick Ungar, 1977.

This volume contains critical reviews of both primary and secondary sources. The reviews span a number of years; some include historical information and some do not. In general, the selections are short and their focus is broad. The individual selections do not appear to be organized in any particular order but each review is complete. The reviews represent comments which were printed at the time of the novel's publication or after the novel regained sufficient popularity with the reading public. The reviews may be of some use to the student who is trying to gain a general sense of the effects produced by Hardy's works.

Vigar, Penelope. *The Novels of Thomas Hardy: Illusion and Reality.* London: The Athlone Press, 1974.

Early in her work, Vigar makes the observation that "What is interesting, and indisputable, is that Hardy's novels, regardless of their chronological position, show enormous variations in intention and execution. . . . "(1). In chapter 1, she identifies what she feels is Hardy's conception of his own art and discusses how his ideas are reflected within the major fiction. Next, Vigar describes features of Hardy's technique that render much of his work successful, but she follows with a chapter devoted to those works that have been classified as experiments or mistakes. The remaining chapters are devoted to individual discussions of the major fiction, with the exclusion of *The Woodlanders*, which is discussed in chapter 2.

Weber, Carl J., comp. *The First Hundred Years of Thomas Hardy 1840-1940: A Centenary Bibliography of Hardiana.* Waterville: Colby College Library, 1942.

The bibliography compiled by Weber is comprehensive in that it provides a nearly complete list of works written about Hardy within the time period of 1840 to 1940. However, there is little or no commentary or evaluation of the works listed, and Hardy's own works are not included. Nevertheless, the bibliography is useful because of its scope.

Widdowson, Peter. *Thomas Hardy.* Plymouth, OK: Northcote House, 1996.

Widdowson's study of Thomas Hardy is useful because he discusses the significance of Hardy's works today. While providing some background material and briefly describing the time period within which Hardy lived, Widdowson goes on to discuss how Hardy's works are being interpreted in the mid-1990's. Also provided prior to the discussion of current critical evaluation of Hardy's work is information regarding the criticism of Hardy's works by contemporaries. This, as stated, is followed by Widdowson's evaluation of Hardy's novels in light of current criticism. The purpose of Widdowson's discussion of the novels is to examine "the appropriateness of using satire to define the fiction. . . by seeing how it can accommodate *all* the novels, and all the elements within all the novels" (32). While Widdowson's approach to the novels is interesting, it is a bit broad in scope to be handled within a single chapter. Yet his comments are useful to those who wish to find a common link among Hardy's novels. In the final chapter of the book, Widdowson discusses Hardy's career as a poet. When read in conjunction with the preceding chapter, the two form an interesting backdrop against which to evaluate Hardy's works.

Wilson, Keith. *Thomas Hardy on Stage*. New York: St. Martin's Press, 1995.

Wilson's book provides readers with a wide range of interesting and useful information. He begins with a discussion of Hardy's interest in drama as well as Hardy's views regarding its use as a vehicle for artistic expression. Wilson also identifies various performances that Hardy had the opportunity to witness and describes how they may have influenced his own dramatic adaptations. One chapter of special interest is that which provides information on the origin and development of the Hardy Players. This group grew out of the local debating society and would later produce numerous adaptations of Hardy's work. Wilson points out that Hardy took a definite interest in their performances and would often make his preferences known with regard to the casting of a particular drama. Wilson lists and describes the adaptations that were made of the novels and poems, and concludes his study with a chapter discussing in detail the stage adaptations of *Tess of the d'Urbervilles*. Also included in this chapter is information about Hardy's relationship with the actress Gertrude Bugler. Wilson notes that she was Mr. Hardy's choice for the role of Tess and that this choice created tension between himself and his second wife, Florence. Florence's relationship with Gertrude is also discussed, as is the production of the play itself. In general, Wilson's book provides readers with information on a less well-known facet of Hardy's career. The information is well organized and the book is enjoyable to read.

Wotton, George. *Thomas Hardy: Towards a Materialist Criticism*. Totowa, New Jersey: Gill & Macmillan, 1985.

Like many critics, Wotton begins his discussion of Hardy and his works by providing readers with information regarding the time period in which Hardy lived. He describes the economy of Dorset and addresses the significant changes brought about in rural communities by the Industrial Revolution. In section three of Part I, titled "The Ideology of the Thinking World and the Production of Wessex," Wotton suggests that "we think of Wessex as a complex system of relations," the most important of which is that "between individuals and that world mediated by work" (41). Throughout his study, Wotton examines the criticism of Hardy's contemporaries as well as that of modern writers. Although Wotton expresses his views consistently throughout his book and in a logical manner, it is difficult to accept some of his principal arguments. However, those who favor a materialistic interpretation of Hardy's works may disagree.

Wright, Reg., ed. *Two English Masters: Charles Dickens and Thomas Hardy*. New York: Marshall Cavendish, 1989.

This oversize book devotes nearly 50 pages to the life and works of Thomas Hardy. Each page contains a variety of color illustrations and photographs which are accompanied by captions that explain their significance. Also included are brief synopses of each of Hardy's major novels, as well as a discussion of some of his poems. Following each discussion of a particular novel are sidebars which list and describe each of the principal characters in the work. These sections are particularly helpful because they assist the reader in recalling important characters and traits which are essential to a clear understanding of each piece. Historical and biographical information is also presented and possible "sources of inspiration" are identified. Overall, the half of the volume devoted to Hardy and his works is informative and very well presented.

The River Frome (Froom) near Lower Bockhampton, Dorset: "The river slid along noiselessly as a shade—the swelling reeds and sedge forming a flexible palisade upon its moist brink" (Chapter XIX, *Far from the Madding Crowd*).

Chapter III
Far from the Madding Crowd

Circumstances of Composition

It is generally agreed that it was *Far from the Madding Crowd* that firmly established Hardy's career as a novelist. Part of the novel's success can be attributed to the distinctly rural setting and to the creation of a fictional world which would continue to grow and develop throughout many of Hardy's later novels. In Michael Millgate's *Hardy: His Career as a Novelist*, Millgate states:

> *Far from the Madding Crowd* developed the presentation of Casterbridge and Budmouth, introduced a number of minor settings, created the village of Weatherbury in all the rich variety of its agricultural life, and introduced the name Wessex into Hardy's fiction for the first time. (235)

In addition to establishing a fictional region which would reappear in later novels, it was in writing *Far from the Madding Crowd* that Hardy seemed to find the "pattern of organization subsequently repeated in all of the most frequently read of his novels" (Gatrell xiii). This pattern is one in which "the narrative structure is developed around one character" (Gatrell xiii).

Although Bathsheba Everdene emerges as the central character, it seems that originally Hardy's conception of the novel involved three central characters. In correspondence to his future editor, Leslie Stephen, Hardy mentioned that the novel could be described as pastoral, and R. L. Purdy identifies Hardy's remarks as having been " 'the chief characters would probably be a young woman-farmer, a shepherd, and a sergeant in the Dragoon Guards' " (Purdy 16). Yet, as the serial version of the novel began to take shape, other characters were added and many of the events began to focus specifically around Bathsheba and the development of her character as she progressed from young girl to mature woman.

Other types of changes in the original design of the novel seem to have occurred as well. At this point in his career, Hardy was very concerned about his personal success as a writer, and he was greatly encouraged by Leslie Stephen's offer to publish his next work. As a result, Hardy was willing to make changes in the manuscript in order to render the novel suitable for publication in serial form. In the article " 'A Good Hand at a Serial': Thomas Hardy and the Serialization of *Far from the Madding Crowd*, " Lawrence Jones outlines several types of changes that Hardy made in order to ensure the novel's success. The areas of primary concern were the Victorian reading audience's sensitivity to sexual elements, the necessity of limiting passages that did not serve to move the action along or help build a strong plot, and the specific arrangement of incidents so that the interest level of the audience would be maintained (Jones 320-321).

One interesting aspect of the many alterations made by Hardy is that the changes, for the most part, do not detract from the overall quality of the story as similar types of changes in later novels seem to have done. Jones goes so far as to say that "The various cuts to speed the action likewise seem not to have harmed the novel and may actually have improved it" (Jones 323). Hardy scholars Michael Millgate and Richard Purdy point out that while Hardy may have felt that the criticisms offered by Leslie Stephen throughout the composition process were excessive or unnecessary, in reality they proved to be extremely important to the novel's success (Purdy 15, Millgate 81), and when "*Far from the Madding Crowd* was first published in the prestigious London *Cornhill* magazine from January to December 1874" (Gatrell xxx) the reviews of the book were very favorable. It was even suggested, because the novel was published anonymously, that perhaps the author of the tale could have been George Eliot, but when Hardy's "identity as the author of *Far from the Madding Crowd* had been revealed in the *Spectator* of 7 February 1874, he soon began to receive approaches from editors and publishers" (Millgate 161).

One extremely interesting facet relating to the composition process is that Hardy apparently felt it was essential for him to be in a specific location while writing the novel. Purdy says that "*Far from the Madding Crowd* was wholly written at Higher Bockhampton" (16), and Millgate describes a letter that Hardy wrote to Leslie Stephen expressing "his desire to stay in Bockhampton until the novel was finished" (Millgate 153). This points out that Hardy believed that it was to his advantage to be near those from whom he was drawing inspiration for his work. The novel certainly reflects Hardy's interest in local happenings and local people. Scenes like the memorable sheep shearing in chapter 12 where the ancient barn is described as something of a timeless feature upon the landscape creates a vivid and enduring image in the mind of the reader. Other scenes which spring from Hardy's personal observations and experiences are also memorable. In reaching out to his own environment for his source of inspiration, Hardy created a novel that "displays throughout the excitement and assurance of a writer who has been given his great opportunity—serialization in the *Cornhill*—at the moment when he begins to realize his proper subject" (Millgate 80). Nevertheless, it was not without effort that Hardy was able to achieve this significant success.

Robert C. Schweik, in "The Early Development of Hardy's *Far from the Madding Crowd*," argues that Hardy's original conception of the novel was somewhat different from what eventually appeared in the serial installments throughout the year 1874. In addition to noting interesting details, such as Oak's name having been changed 12 times and that Poorheed at some point became Poorhead (422-423), Schweik is able to show how changes in foliation in the Cornhill manuscript indicate various significant changes in plot and character development.

Works Cited

Gatrell, Simon. Introduction. *Far from the Madding Crowd.* By Thomas Hardy. New York: Oxford University Press, 1993. xiii-xxviii, xxx.

Jones, Lawrence. " 'A Good Hand at a Serial': Thomas Hardy and the Serialization of *Far from the Madding Crowd*." *Studies in the Novel* 10.3 (1978): 320-334.

Millgate, Michael. *Thomas Hardy: A Biography.* New York: Random House, 1982.

Purdy, Richard L. *Thomas Hardy: A Bibliographical Study.* Oxford: Clarendon Press, 1968.

Schweik, Robert C. "The Early Development of Hardy's *Far from the Madding Crowd.*" *Texas Studies in Literature and Language* 9 (1967): 414-428.

Jones, Lawrence. " 'A Good Hand at a Serial': Thomas Hardy and the Serialization of *Far from the Madding Crowd.*" *Studies in the Novel* 10.3 (1978): 320-334.

Jones begins by outlining several types of changes that Hardy made to ensure the novel's success. The areas of primary concern were the Victorian reading audience's sensitivity to incidents in the plot involving sexual elements, the necessity of limiting passages that did not serve to move the action along or to help build a strong plot, and the specific arrangement of incidents so that the interest level of the audience would be maintained (320-321). Later in the article Jones refers to a variety of suggestions made by Leslie Stephen to Hardy regarding the relationship between Fanny and Troy as well as the existence of their child (321-322). He describes several omissions in addition to various changes in language made by Hardy in direct response to Stephen's concerns. In discussing passages deleted for the purpose of condensing the action, Jones says "The various cuts to speed the action likewise seem not to have harmed the novel and may actually have improved it" (323). He goes on to point out that throughout the novel there are various "indications of Hardy's anxiety to create a magazine story full of incident" (325). To support his assertions, Jones includes examples from the text as printed in the *Cornhill* as well as the manuscript and the *Wessex* editions of 1912. He is careful to mention that even in 1912, 38 years after the initial publication, Hardy continued to make substantial revisions in the work.

Millgate, Michael. *Thomas Hardy: His Career as a Novelist.* New York: St. Martin's Press, 1994.

In Part Two, titled "Achievement," of Millgate's book, he discusses the period in Hardy's career where he began to experience success as a novelist. Millgate points to the novel *Far from the Madding Crowd* as the novel that

> displays throughout the excitement and assurance of a writer who has been given his great opportunity—serialization in the *Cornhill*—at the moment when he begins to realize his proper subject. (80)

He continues by describing the novel's circumstances of composition and by examining the influence of editorial comments on the text. Also addressed are specific incidents in the plot and the addition of Boldwood's character somewhat late in the composition process. Hardy's interest in depicting scenes from an unusual point of view is also discussed. Millgate concludes his study of *Far from the Madding Crowd* with an analysis of the behavior of the central characters with particular emphasis on Bathsheba Everdene and Gabriel Oak. This selection provides a great deal of information regarding the novel and serves as a foundation piece upon which readers can build further study. Millgate's work is presented in a manner that is particularly useful to the general reader as well as to the scholar.

Schweik, Robert C. "The Early Development of Hardy's *Far from the Madding Crowd.*" *Texas Studies in Literature and Language* 9 (1967): 414-428.

This article provides much information about the early phases of the composition of *Far from the Madding Crowd.* Schweik discusses the development of the manuscript as later printed in the *Cornhill* throughout the year 1874. He asserts that Hardy's original conception of the novel was somewhat different from what eventually appeared in the serial installments. As a result of a thorough examination of the *Cornhill* manuscript, Schweik is able to show how changes in foliation reveal various significant changes in plot and character development. He also cites letters written by Leslie Stephen, editor of the *Cornhill*, to Hardy regarding specific revisions in the text. Further, Schweik argues that evidence from the letters and evidence provided in the manuscript indicate "that the Boldwood episodes and the dramatizations of Fanny Robin's story were probably not part of Hardy's first version of the novel" (426). This is an important observation because both Fanny and Boldwood add a dimension to the novel that would certainly be missing without them. Also, the various descriptions of Fanny's and Boldwood's circumstances serve to render the overall tone of the novel as being more sympathetic to the plight of each of the characters involved in the events which transpire as a result of their interaction with one another. Schweik says:

> By adding the dramatizations of Fanny Robin's story and developing Boldwood as another major character, Hardy laid the groundwork for a broader treatment of feeling than was possible within the conventional love triangle with which he had begun . . . (427-428).

The overall success of the novel appears to substantiate the view that the changes made by Hardy improved the quality of the novel, and as Schweik successfully points out, the changes reveal that Hardy actually altered his conception of the novel throughout the composition process.

Schweik, Robert C. "An Error in the Text of Hardy's *Far from the Madding Crowd.*" *Colby Library Quarterly* VII.6 (1966): 269.

Schweik identifies a typesetting error which occurred in the 1895 edition of the novel. Apparently the word "simulated" was changed to "stimulated" in a sentence describing Fanny Robin's reaction to her dire circumstances. Within the context of the sentence the word "simulated" is more consistent with the ideas being expressed. The error occurs in chapter XL.

Schweik, Robert C. "A First Draft Chapter of Hardy's *Far from the Madding Crowd.*" *English Studies* 53 (1972): 344-349.

Schweik describes in detail a chapter from the original manuscript of *Far from the Madding Crowd*. He describes the foliation of the pages and provides an explanation for their omission in the fair copy that was used by the *Cornhill Magazine*. Schweik says:

> What is most immediately striking about this canceled chapter is what it suggests about some major revisions which Hardy must have made—most notably in character and character relationships—between the first draft and the Fair copy version of the novel. (23)

He refers specifically to Hardy's revisions relating to Gabriel Oak who was, in the initial draft, Bathsheba's employee rather than an independent farmer. Other revisions involve the development of Troy and his relationship to Oak. Schweik argues that overall, Hardy's revisions improved the quality of the story as well as the authenticity of the characters.

Springer, Marlene. *Hardy's Use of Allusion*. Lawrence: University Press of Kansas, 1983.

Chapter 3 of Springer's text is especially informative to readers of *Far from the Madding Crowd* because, here, she describes both the circumstances of composition and the critical reception of the novel. Also discussed is the development of *Wessex* as a fictional region and the development of various themes and conflicts within the novel. In addition, Springer writes about Hardy's use of irony as it grew and developed throughout the early novels. Finally, Springer addresses Hardy's use of allusion. She says, "As Hardy paints his *Wessex* and explores these new psychological levels he once again turns to allusion to reveal, enlarge, intensify and solemnize" (57). She identifies over 150 allusions in *Far from the Madding Crowd* and goes on to describe the effectiveness of Hardy's technique. Numerous examples are provided, and Springer's discussion is enlightening and easy to follow.

Windram, William T. "A Discrepancy in *Far from the Madding Crowd." Notes and Queries* 29.4 (1982): 326.

This very brief selection identifies a contradiction in two statements regarding the respective ages of two principal characters. Windram points out that the narrator gives Gabriel's age as twenty-eight but that there is one reference to Gabriel as being six years older than Bathsheba and another to his being eight years her senior. Windram attributes the discrepancy to an oversight by Hardy during the revision process.

Comparative Studies

Beatty, C. J. P. "Thomas Hardy and Thomas Hughes." *English Studies* 68 (1987): 511-518.

In general, Beatty explores Hardy's use of the term *Wessex* and takes issue with those who would credit Hardy as being the first to use the term in fictional writings. Beatty cites the work of writer Thomas Hughes and his novel *Tom Brown's School Days* as providing evidence that Hughes used the term prior to Hardy. Later in the article, Beatty identifies and describes various characters, settings, and themes which he finds to be similar in the works of Thomas Hardy and Thomas Hughes. Although the majority of comparisons discussed involve a comparison between *Jude the Obscure* (Hardy) and *Tom Brown at Oxford* (Hughes), there are several references to *Far from the Madding Crowd*. Specifically, Beatty refers to Hardy's own claim in the preface to *Far from the Madding Crowd* where Hardy himself writes that he believes he is responsible for bringing the term *Wessex* into popular use.

Draper, Ronald P. "Introduction to the Case Book. Thomas Hardy: Three Pastoral Novels." *The Thomas Hardy Journal* 4.1 (1988): 36-49.

Draper begins with a discussion of Hardy's vision of the pastoral and then provides some brief detail regarding the composition of the early novels. Also discussed is the early critical reception of *Under the Greenwood Tree* and *Far from the Madding Crowd*. Later in the article Draper begins to draw comparisons between the two novels in terms of structure and theme. Next, Draper discusses the relationship of *The Woodlanders* to *Under the Greenwood Tree* and *Far from the Madding Crowd*. The following portion of the article deals primarily with the evaluations of more current critical interpretations of the novels. Draper summarizes and evaluates the positions taken by numerous critics who address the similarities between and among *Under the Greenwood Tree*, *Far from the Madding Crowd*, and *The Woodlanders*. Draper states that criticism of the novels can be divided into two categories, comic and tragic. Draper seems to view *Under the Greenwood Tree* and *Far from the Madding Crowd* as being more optimistic than *The Woodlanders*, and concludes the article by providing an example from the text of *Far from the Madding Crowd* that he feels best defines Hardy's interpretation of the term *pastoral*.

Grimsditch, Herbert B. *Character and Environment in the Novels of Thomas Hardy*. 1925. New York: Russell and Russell, 1962.

Grimsditch refers to *Far from the Madding Crowd* at numerous points throughout his book. The bulk of his comments concerning *Far from the Madding Crowd* can be found in chapter VII, titled "Occupation." The focus of his comments relating to this particular novel has to do with its rural setting. Grimsditch states "*Far from the Madding Crowd* is the most complete picture of farm life Hardy has given us" (160). He goes on to discuss the significance of Bathsheba's role within the farming environment and points out that while Bathsheba is successful in business, she is unable to transfer this success to her personal relationships. Grimsditch also discusses both Gabriel Oak's and Farmer Boldwood's roles as agricultural workers. He describes their personal characteristics and explains how these characteristics help determine the course of action each man chooses personally and professionally. Also in chapter VII are descriptions of various other characters from the *Wessex* novels. A variety of comparisons are drawn between and among the characters which help the reader to better understand the novels as a group.

Jones, Lawrence. " 'Infected by a Vein of Mimeticism': George Eliot and the Technique of *Far from the Madding Crowd.*" *The Journal of Narrative Technique* 8 (1978): 56-76.

In this article, Jones addresses a topic that is frequently, if briefly, mentioned throughout Hardy criticism. Jones is attempting to show that Hardy was definitely influenced by the works of George Eliot and that he was influenced in a variety of areas. One area of influence appears in Hardy's presentation of verbal pictures or paintings modeled after the paintings of Dutch realists. Jones argues that this is the same type of technique used by George Eliot in the novel *Adam Bede*. He goes on to say, "The similarity of the pictorial handling of the rural setting is especially striking if one compares the description of the Hall Farm in *Adam Bede* with the Everdene homestead" (60). Jones uses this statement to begin to explain how the use of verbal pictures also influences the ways in which both authors develop the characters in each of their novels. In addition, Jones provides many examples from the texts of *Far from the Madding Crowd* and *Adam Bede*. The examples are generally used to show similarities in descriptive passages, character development, and similar use of metaphor and diction. The article is very interesting and provides readers with much information regarding the basis for the frequent references in Hardy criticism to the relationship between the novels written by Eliot and Hardy.

Sasaki, Toru. "On Boldwood's Retina: A 'Moment of Vision' in *Far from the Madding Crowd* and Its Possible Relation to *Middlemarch.*" *The Thomas Hardy Journal* 8 (1992): 57-60.

Several topics are discussed in this short article by Sasaki. Primarily three areas are addressed: 1) the theme of possession, 2) the motif of branding, and 3) the significance of the color red. Sasaki views these areas as threads that run throughout the novel and contribute to its overall development. Sasaki also discusses Hardy's particular use of the word *retina* and relates his use of the term in *A Pair of Blue Eyes* and *Far from the Madding Crowd* to George Eliot's use of the same term in *Middlemarch*. While reluctant to assert that Thomas Hardy was actually familiar with Eliot's *Middlemarch*, Sasaki does make the point that similar use of the term is employed and the presence of similar themes among the novels does exist. However, the article is a bit brief and could be more fully developed.

Shelston, Alan. " 'Were they Beautiful?': *Far from the Madding Crowd* and *Daniel Deronda*." *The Thomas Hardy Journal* 81 (1992): 65-67.

This brief article discusses the influence Hardy's writing may have had on George Eliot's. Shelston points out that while many have compared the work of Hardy to that of Eliot in order to establish Eliot's influence upon Hardy, few have examined the converse. When looking at *Far from the Madding Crowd* and *Daniel Deronda*, he says, "What seems not sufficiently to have been considered is that George Eliot herself may have read Hardy's novel, and have done so at a particularly significant moment in her own career" (65). Shelston then presents information regarding the circumstances of composition of each of the two novels. He does this to substantiate his claims that it is possible for Eliot to have been reading *Far from the Madding Crowd* at the time she was working on *Daniel Deronda*. The article is brief but interesting and, as stated, challenges those who would attribute the borrowing of ideas and/or style to Hardy alone.

Stottlar, James F. "Hardy vs. Pinero: Two Stage Versions of *Far from the Madding Crowd*." *Theatre Survey* 28.2 (1977): 23-43.

This article is an interesting discussion of the stage adaptations of Hardy's *Far from the Madding Crowd*. As Stottlar points out in the title of his article, two versions of the play were produced—one being that prepared by Hardy and his associate Joseph Comyns Carr and the other being the version written by Arthur Wing Pinero. Although there was a great deal of controversy relating to the similarities between the two plays and the possible borrowing of ideas by Pinero, Stottlar's primary interest is in what caused Pinero's version to be more successful than Hardy's. Stottlar attributes the success of Pinero's adaptation, titled *The Squire*, to the type of audience that was attending theatrical productions at the time. He argues that Hardy and Carr failed to recognize the changes that were taking place in drama and that as a result "they worked up striking situations, exciting episodes, impressive scenic displays, violence, broad contrasts, and heightened effects" (27). These elements were apparently no longer popular among Victorian theatre audiences, and since Pinero's version was a much more subtle presentation of a similar story, it became the more successful rendering of the two. In addition to drawing comparisons between the two plays,

Stottlar compares the novel *Far from the Madding Crowd* to Hardy's stage adaptation. He provides examples from the text of the novel as well as the scripts of both plays. His observations are useful and informative, and the article is well organized and not difficult to read.

Nature of the Novel

Eastman, Ronald. "Time and Propriety in *Far from the Madding Crowd*." *Interpretations* 10 (1978): 20-33.

Eastman discusses the significance of time as expressed in Hardy's novels as a group and *Far from the Madding Crowd* in particular. He describes in some detail Gabriel Oak's relationship to and interest in time. He refers specifically to the well-known and often quoted passage describing the great barn. Eastman states, "The harmony between time past and time present which the barn houses and over which Oak presides represents Hardy's ideal of temporality and community" (25). Further, Eastman argues that the major conflict in the novel is directly related to "the propitious use of time" (26). He contrasts the behaviors of Frank Troy and Bathsheba Everdene to those of Gabriel Oak, pointing out that while Gabriel has a proper sense of time, Bathsheba and Troy do not. Finally, Eastman refers to the narrator's knowledge of time as giving power and substance to the novel.

Fisher, Joe. *The Hidden Hardy*. New York: St. Martin's Press, 1992.

Fisher looks individually as well as collectively at nine of Hardy's novels. He argues that within each individual novel there exists a counter-text which serves the purpose of perpetuating a specific ideology. Chapter 2 is devoted to a discussion of *Far from the Madding Crowd* and is based upon Fisher's notion that an identifiable counter-text is present within its framework. He views the creation of *Wessex* as somehow being a tool that Hardy used to gain power over his readers. Also, he states that "the necessary credulousness of the reader in this situation, able to judge only the veracity of the bourgeois parable the characters play out, gives Hardy further power over its text and its reproduction" (39). Moreover, Fisher finds fault with Hardy's plot structure and character development. In considering the characters, Fisher finds the roles of all three of Bathsheba's suitors very problematic, and he even goes so far as to say that the particular attributes given to Oak, Troy, and Boldwood are a "part of Hardy's covert sexualization of his text" (44). Later in the article, Fisher talks about Hardy's use of allusion as well as various symbols. In general, Fisher's arguments are pejorative in tone and are difficult to follow. Although the notion of a sub-text is interesting, it seems as if the scope of Fisher's arguments is a bit far reaching.

Jagdish, Chandra Dave. *The Human Predicament in Hardy's Novels*. London: Macmillan, 1985.

Although Jagdish's book is somewhat complicated in its overall presentation, certain portions of the work are of special interest to readers of *Far from the Madding Crowd*. Since Jagdish looks at "Hardy's vision of the world as manifested in a series of his novels" (3), a knowledge of several of Hardy's works is helpful to the reader. A section on *Far from the Madding Crowd* can be found in Part II, titled "The Establishment of Harmony: Hardy's Ethical Resolution of the Metaphysical Absurd." Within this part, sections four and seven provide interesting insights into the development of Hardy's characters in general, and the development of Gabriel Oak in particular. In describing Oak, Jagdish states:

> He is a picture of rusticity and rugged candour who appears, at first, comical . . . but his greatness blossoms under the impact of adversity as he strides from the state of inertia prior to his awakening into the human predicament, to the serenity surpassing the strain of revolt. (71)

Jagdish continues by explaining how Oak represents a specific line in Hardy's thinking and compares Oak's actions to those of various other characters in the novel. A close reading is necessary because of the theoretical terminology used in the article, and a knowledge of the major works is helpful even when reading an individual section of Jagdish's book.

Meisel, Perry. *Thomas Hardy: The Return of the Repressed*. New Haven, CT: Yale University Press, 1972.

Meisel essentially examines Hardy's major works and states that "the primary characteristic of his fiction is its tension—a tension that permeates the development of his universe on prose and that lends a distinctly historical aspect to this work" (1). He discusses *Far from the Madding Crowd* in relation to two additional novels (*Under the Greenwood Tree* and *A Pair of Blue Eyes*) that Hardy wrote early in his career as a novelist. Meisel stresses the importance of examining the three early novels because they provide a firm foundation upon which Hardy was to build a successful career. He goes so far as to say that "Hardy's early work defines the distinctively individual aspects of his creations" (32). Within the chapter devoted to the examination of Hardy's early works, Meisel not only looks at the conflicts that exist within each novel, but he also describes the creation of *Wessex*, provides biographical information about Hardy, and addresses various themes as well as the development of many characters. Numerous examples from the texts of the novels are provided and somewhat lengthy descriptions of the principal characters are present. The chapter provides readers with a great deal of useful information regarding *Far from the Madding Crowd* as well as the other early novels.

Schweik, Robert C. "The Narrative Structure of *Far from the Madding Crowd*." *Budmouth Essays on Thomas Hardy*. Ed. F. B. Pinion. Dorchester: The Thomas Hardy Society, 1976. 21-38.

In a brief preface to his essay, Schweik argues against those who would assert "that Hardy's novels can safely be discussed as if they were unified narrative constructs" (21). He further explains the importance of examining the composition process for elements that may help explain shifts in narrative manner or technique. Schweik discusses the nature of several publications and describes how the novel began to take shape. He begins by looking at the first five chapters of the novel and says that "frequent shifting and balancing of attitudes towards his subject is characteristic of Hardy's manner throughout the first five chapters" (23). Schweik continues by describing how Hardy's initial variations in tone made it difficult for him to continue the novel. He also points out that revisions were made throughout the composition process, indicating that Hardy's method was likely one of improvisation rather than deliberate planning. The points made by Schweik are significant and are helpful in providing readers with a better understanding of the novel.

Shelston, Alan. "The Particular Pleasure of *Far from the Madding Crowd*." *The Thomas Hardy Yearbook* 7 (1977): 31-39.

In this selection Shelston describes the reactions of two of Hardy's contemporaries, Henry James and D. H. Lawrence, to *Far from the Madding Crowd*. He stresses that their criticism of the work emphasizes interpretation and evaluation based upon their own personal views regarding the proper methodology used in novel writing. Shelston argues that the effect that the work produces is of equal importance and explains why he feels reading *Far from the Madding Crowd* provides readers with a pleasurable experience. Specifically, Shelston mentions Hardy's use of color. He says "constantly throughout the novel we are made aware of the impact of colour" (34). Shelston goes on to provide examples that serve to illustrate this point and further says that the use of color "is an important factor in Hardy's self-communicating narrative delight" (34). Overall, Shelston feels that the pleasurable effects produced by reading the novel stem from Hardy's effective control of the narrative. This observation is consistent with the views of many critics who argue that Hardy was very nearly at his best when writing *Far from the Madding Crowd*.

Squires, Michael. "*Far from the Madding Crowd* as Modified Pastoral." *Nineteenth-Century Fiction* 25.3 (1970): 299-326.

Beginning with a discussion of the term *pastoral* and providing the definitions given by several critics, Squires goes on to create what he feels is a current interpretation of the term. He defines the term *pastoral* as the genre of literature

> which idealizes country life through the sharp contrast between city and country, the implied withdrawal from a complex to a simple world, the urban awareness of rural life and the resulting tension between value systems . . . (303)

Squires then provides evidence to support his assertion that *Far from the Madding Crowd* is a modified rather than traditional pastoral. He thoroughly examines the plot of the novel and also addresses the significance of theme. Interspersed throughout the article are lengthy examples from the text. These examples serve to illustrate essential elements in plot and setting as well as Hardy's rendering of theme. Squires praises Hardy's narrative technique and his observations serve to guide readers to a clearer interpretation of the novel.

Viera, Carroll. "The Name Levi in *Far from the Madding Crowd*." *The Thomas Hardy Yearbook* 14 (1987): 63.

This brief discussion of the significance of the name Levi helps to shed light on some of the more intricate elements of the novel. By tracing the origin of the name to its association with the Bible, Viera is able to show how Hardy may have used the name in order to establish more firmly the tension between the rural and urban elements in Bathsheba's character. Viera asserts that since Bathsheba's father Levi was said to have been from the city, Hardy used the name "in order to subtly convey some of the traits which Bathsheba has inherited from her parent" (63). The traits associated with Bathsheba and her urban family are those of *vanity*, *artfulness*, and *artifice*. Viera concludes by describing *Far from the Madding Crowd* as a pastoral novel and points out that the use of the name Levi is just one of the many elements Hardy used to help create a sense of tension between the rural and urban characters in the novel.

Webster, Roger. "Reproducing Hardy: Familiar and Unfamiliar Versions of *Far from the Madding Crowd* and *Tess of the d'Urbervilles.*" *Critical Survey* 5.2 (1993): 143-151.

Webster states that in his essay he wants to "consider the ways in which Hardy's novels have been treated in their critical reception and history, and how the film versions of *Far from the Madding Crowd* and *Tess of the d'Urbervilles* relate to this process" (144)" The early portion of the article is devoted to a discussion of the tendency of critics to interpret Hardy's novels as a group rather than individually. Webster also explains that since the novels have become part of the British culture, the tendency to oversimplify criticism has occurred. Further, he would argue that often a reader's response to a given novel can be somewhat predetermined by prior knowledge of the popular criticism. Webster relates this specifically to the film adaptations by saying, "Hardy's novels translate very effectively into a cinematic medium: the visual dimension and features of the narrative provide excellent material for cinematic equivalents" (147). This being the case, he argues, it is important to examine the film as an independent text. Webster poses questions about the reasoning behind making film adaptations of novels in general, and specific novels like *Far from the Madding Crowd* and *Tess of the d'Urbervilles* in particular. He talks about the time period in which the movies were filmed (1967 and 1980 respectively) and concludes that while the films themselves may have been successful, each is an example of the tendency to simplify Hardy's work.

Welsh, James M. "Hardy and the Pastoral, Schlesinger and Shepherds: *Far from the Madding Crowd.*" *Literature and Film Quarterly* 9.2 (1981): 79-84.

Welsh provides commentary on John Schlesinger's film version of *Far from the Madding Crowd*. He argues that it is only partially successful because the novel is "greatly compressed and much diluted" (79). Welsh goes on to discuss how the major characters are portrayed on screen and expresses his disappointment with the oversimplification of the interpretations of Bathsheba Everdene, Gabriel Oak, Sergeant Troy, and Farmer Boldwood. Later in the article he refers to significant scenes from the novel that do not appear anywhere in the film. Nevertheless, Welsh points out that there are certain difficulties in adapting a novel to the screen and that if viewed for entertainment purposes, the film is enjoyable to watch.

Salient Features of the Novel

Babb, Howard. "Setting and Theme in *Far from the Madding Crowd*." *English Literary History* 30 (1963): 147-161.

Babb begins his article by stressing the importance of setting in Hardy's fiction. He asserts that *Far from the Madding Crowd* illustrates "with something of the obviousness of a textbook—how setting can be used to reinforce and indeed at times render theme" (147). In attempting to show just how the setting is used to express the major theme of the novel, he refers to the characters, their names, and their relationship to nature. In arguing that "at bottom, Hardy's story juxtaposes two different worlds or modes of being" (148), Babb identifies Gabriel, Bathsheba, Boldwood, Troy, and Fanny as the central characters. He describes each of the characters in relationship to the setting in which each is introduced. Further, he suggests that nature can be viewed as being sympathetic to the characters that are most closely allied with the earth in terms of personality and profession. The article captures the reader's attention, yet it fails in clarity at some points. Babb seems to be suggesting the existence of the use of objective correlatives to reinforce theme, but he does not employ the term. However, the examples cited from the text of the novel in terms of setting merit examination in the format he suggests.

Bullen, J. B. "Thomas Hardy's *Far from the Madding Crowd*: Perception and Understanding." *The Thomas Hardy Journal* 3.2 (1987): 38-61.

In this analysis of *Far from the Madding Crowd*, Bullen examines the effects of Victorian psychological theory on Hardy's writing. Bullen refers specifically to perception theory and the works of Ruskin. Bullen states:

> Ruskin's emphasis on the penetrative power of the visual imagination gained support from psychology, philosophy, and literary criticism, and Hardy must have felt openly encouraged to explore various ways of articulating a visual response which came quite naturally to him. (42)

Later, Bullen addresses the theme of the "relationship between seeing and understanding" within the novel and describes the opportunities various characters have of viewing each other. Bullen stresses the importance of observations made by characters such as Gabriel and Bathsheba and explains how their particular perceptions of each other develop as a result of these observations. Near the end of the article, Bullen returns to a discussion of psychology and philosophy as sources of inspiration for Hardy. He concludes by stating that *Far from the Madding Crowd* can be evaluated on a variety of levels without detracting from the overall quality of the work.

Cornwell-Robinson, Margery. "Of Cows and Catfish: The Reading of Nature by Thomas Hardy and Loren Eiseley." *Soundings* 68 (1985): 52-61.

This article is somewhat unusual in its approach in that Cornwell-Robinson compares the works of Loren Eiseley, an archeologist and an evolutionist, to those of Thomas Hardy. She looks specifically at the ways in which both authors observe and describe nature and/or natural phenomenon. After examining various writings by both Hardy and Eiseley, Cornwell-Robinson makes several observations:

> Eiseley and Hardy have concluded that careful and constant familiarity with the commonplace in nature emphasizes the mysteries from which the special human animal has sprung and which this creature must still accept. (54)

Although some of her observations are interesting, and she does make numerous references to *Far from the Madding Crowd*, the general premise of the article is a bit underdeveloped.

Goss, Michael. "Aspects of Time in *Far from the Madding Crowd*."
    The Thomas Hardy Journal 6.3 (1990): 43-53.
    Goss begins his article by distinguishing between Hardy's use of time
as measured by a clock and *time* in the universal sense. Also discussed
is Hardy's use of the description of sound that serves to draw attention
to intense silence. Further, Goss explains that the elements of sound,
being absent or present, often signify the passage of time relating to
individual characters. To support his arguments, Goss provides the
example of Fanny's missed appointment with Troy and Gabriel's use of
a watch that he cannot depend upon to keep time accurately. In
addition, he mentions the maltster who calculates his age based upon
the conditions of his employment. After this series of examples Goss
states, "Time is useful in estimating character because characters'
attitudes to it and how they assess it help us to assess them" (46). In
assessing the various characters on this basis, Goss concludes that while
under the influence of various aspects of time Troy's life deteriorated to
the point of death, Oak and Bathsheba experienced much improvement.

Howe, Irving. *Thomas Hardy*. London: Macmillan, 1967.
    Howe devotes much discussion to *Far from the Madding Crowd* in
various sections of his book. Some of his most interesting and helpful
comments can be found in chapter III, titled "The World of Wessex."
He states that *Far from the Madding Crowd* is

> the first of the Wessex novels to bring into play Hardy's greatest gift as a
> writer of fiction—his gift for those compressed incidents or miniature
> dramas . . . which in a page or two illuminate whole stretches of
> experience. (52)

Howe goes on to describe the novel as one that addresses the problem
of social discipline. He continues to build his argument by explaining
that the major characters, Bathsheba and Gabriel, are defined by "the
work they do or fail to do" (53). Howe also discusses Hardy's
presentation of each of the major characters but maintains that
Bathsheba is the most singular among them. Overall, his observations
are interesting and help the reader to better understand the theme of
discipline within the novel as well as the roles of the various characters.

Nollen, E. M. "The Loving Look in *Far from the Madding Crowd*."
    The Thomas Hardy Yearbook 13 (1986): 69-73.

In this brief article Nollen discusses the theme of sight and the unique perceptions of Oak, Boldwood, and Troy regarding Bathsheba. Nollen also examines Bathsheba's view of love as it relates to the three central male characters and discusses the image of Bathsheba as presented by the author. Nollen goes on to argue that the author's vision of Bathsheba is most closely related to that of Gabriel Oak. Further, Nollen asserts that

> *Far from the Madding Crowd* marks an important stage in Hardy's career, for this is the first and only one of the six major Wessex novels where the author explicitly sanctions a particular vision of love, in this case, that of Gabriel Oak. (73)

This statement indicates the significance of Oak's views as a character and also serves to summarize the major focus of the article.

Reid, Fred. "Art and Ideology in *Far from the Madding Crowd*." *Thomas Hardy Annual* 4 (1986): 91-126.

Reid begins his article with a discussion of various critical approaches that have been applied to Hardy's fiction in general. He continues by describing how the term *pastoral* has changed over time and suggests that a "conservative version of pastoral co-exists in *Far from the Madding Crowd*, with a much older version of the form, a version which can be traced back to early Greek literature" (93). The remaining portion of the article is divided into five additional sections addressing such topics as the agricultural and religious institutions and practices of Dorset at mid-century, the particular beliefs of William Cobbett, and the presence of conflicting ideologies as expressed in the novel *Far from the Madding Crowd*. Reid's arguments are persuasive, and he includes examples from the text of the novel that help support his views. The information is well organized and directs readers toward a more thorough understanding of the novel.

Character Analysis

Adey, Lionel. "Styles of Love in *Far from the Madding Crowd*." *Thomas Hardy Annual* 5 (1987): 47-62.

Adey examines the style or type of love exhibited by the major characters Bathsheba, Sergeant Troy, Gabriel Oak, and Boldwood. He draws on the research of sociologist John Alan Lee, and in doing so, identifies and describes five modes of love. Adey explains how these modes are expressed by the various characters. He would further argue that there is an overall pattern in Hardy's novels which links specific styles of love with certain character traits and actions. He says:

> In Hardy novels Storgic lovers serve and manage land . . . . Manic lovers, driven by their delusions, find themselves always out of phase or bored . . . [and] Ludic love, as many a folk-song implies, pertains to the transient or unstable, to soldiers, rakes, or hucksters. (55)

Next, Adey focuses specifically on Bathsheba and describes how her growth as a character relates directly to her mode of loving. He concludes by arguing that Bathsheba is an interesting and substantial character.

Beegel, Susan. "Bathsheba's Lovers: Male Sexuality in *Far from the Madding Crowd.*" *Tennessee Studies in Literature* 27 (1984): 108-127.

Beegel focuses on the three major male characters of Oak, Troy, and Boldwood. She describes the ways in which they court Bathsheba and talks about the types of passion expressed by each of the men. One scene that she finds particularly enlightening is the scene where Bathsheba witnesses Troy's sword play. A lengthy excerpt from the text is provided. Beegel states that "the scene's real excitement depends on the sword's capacity to deal death" (113). Beegel also discusses Troy's relationship with Fanny, the stillbirth of their illegitimate child, and the subsequent death of Fanny. She goes so far as to give the chapter entitled "The Gargoyle" a sexual interpretation. Later, other lengthy portions of the text are included for the purpose of identifying phallic symbols. Beegel's position is a bit overstated and detracts somewhat from the benefits of a more traditional reading.

Casagrande, Peter J. "A New View of Bathsheba Everdene." *Critical Approaches to the Novels of Thomas Hardy.* Ed. Dale Kramer. London: Macmillan, 1979. 50-73.

In this section Casagrande examines the delineation of Bathsheba's character. He also discusses the role of Gabriel Oak and says that "Oak's prominence is best seen, I think, as a function of Bathsheba's imperfection" (51). Casagrande argues against interpretations that describe Bathsheba's development as occurring naturally over a long period of time. He points out that she is subjected to a series of violent and shocking happenings in a relatively short period of time and that it is these events that seem to precipitate a change in her character rather than simply the passage of time. Somewhat later in his essay Casagrande gives a brief summary of the plot and discusses in straightforward and succinct terms Hardy's portrayal of the major characters. Casagrande comes to the conclusion that the character Bathsheba is evidence of Hardy's view "that women by nature are infirm" (55). He continually refers to Bathsheba's innate weakness as well as to Gabriel's strength. He concludes by stating, "Hardy associates Bathsheba's prescriptive infirmity with the iradicable defect he sees in non-human nature and presents in Oak an example of how to cope with the imperfection of things" (70). Although some of his arguments are plausible, Casagrande's assertions regarding Hardy's beliefs about women are open to further discussion and investigation.

Chalfront, Fran E. "From Strength to Strength: John Schlesinger's Film of *Far from the Madding Crowd.*" *Thomas Hardy Annual* 5 (1987): 63-74.

Chalfront discusses the American and British viewing audiences' response to Schlesinger's film adaptation of *Far from the Madding Crowd.* Chalfront says that while audiences in the 1960's were not particularly enthusiastic, the film is now regarded as a minor classic at least in England and possibly in America as well. Chalfront gives several specific examples of scenes that are presented particularly well in the film. The scenes identified by Chalfront are the missed appointment between Fanny and Frank Troy and the storm scene where Gabriel Oak works to save Bathsheba's harvest. Chalfront also finds the portrayal of William Boldwood to be sympathetic as well as effective. Overall, Chalfront finds the film as faithful as the book in the rendering of theme and in terms of presenting the relationships among the principal characters.

Garson, Marjorie. *Hardy's Fables of Integrity.* Oxford: Clarendon Press, 1991.

Garson sets out to identify the ways in which Hardy's personal beliefs or obsessions work their way into his narratives. Seven novels are discussed individually in chapters titled after the respective novels. In her discussion of *Far from the Madding Crowd*, Garson focuses on the characters and how their roles function in opposition to one another. More specifically, she talks about Gabriel Oak as being the unifying force in the narrative. She says, "Gabriel is the foil to all the other main characters in that although thwarted, he is not self-divided. A mature man when the novel begins, Gabriel is eminently 'together' " (27). While Garson views Gabriel as being *together*, she views Bathsheba as more self-divided than any of the other characters. To support this assertion she cites the fact that Bathsheba possesses traits that liken her to the Goddess Diana as well as those that are similar to those of Venus. She states that "the Venus-Diana split buttresses Hardy's plot" (35). In addition to examining the development of various characters and certain elements in the plot, Garson also discusses theme and imagery. The chapter is of moderate length and the terminology could prove to be problematic for the novice, but Garson's arguments are well stated. She addresses features of the novel that are significant and presents the information in a logically organized manner. Nevertheless, she views the novel as failing in some points, and her stance is in opposition to the views of those who regard this novel as generally successful and unproblematic.

Gatrell, Simon. "*Far from the Madding Crowd* Revisited." *The Thomas Hardy Journal* 10 (1994): 38-50.

Gatrell's article focuses on the representation of the character Gabriel Oak. He suggests that conflicting positions taken by the narrator at many points throughout the story lead to two different interpretations of Gabriel as a character. Gatrell argues that

> The strong, independent Gabriel, who only stays by Bathsheba because he wants to prevent disaster from overtaking the woman he loves, gets lost from time to time behind the figure of the hopeless worshipper, bound to serve whether he will or no. (48)

Throughout the article, Gatrell supplies examples from the text to show the shifts in the narrative voice. Further, he asserts that these shifts occur partly as a result of Hardy's lack of confidence as a writer. Also, Gatrell refers to the correspondence between Hardy and Leslie Stephen (editor of the *Cornhill*) as a source which reveals that various revisions in the plot and methods of characterization were discussed and implemented. In general, Gatrell's arguments are clearly presented and add insight into the development and interpretation of the character Gabriel Oak.

Hyman, Virginia R. *Ethical Perspective in the Novels of Thomas Hardy.* New York: Kennikat Press, 1975.

The two chapters in Hyman's book that are of particular interest to readers of *Far from the Madding Crowd* are chapters 4 and 5. Chapter 4, titled "The Early Novels," provides the reader with insights regarding the gradual development of Hardy's writing technique. Hyman also examines the development of Hardy's value system as it is reflected in his novels. Using this information as a basis for her comments on *Far from the Madding Crowd* in chapter 5, Hyman explores Hardy's presentation of Bathshcba, Oak, Troy, and Boldwood. She discusses the characters in contrast to one another and asserts that through the creation of his characters "what Hardy does in *Far from the Madding Crowd* is to develop new and more subtle ways of expressing his values" (50). Hyman also attempts to explain Hardy's concept of the term *altruism*, and further describes the development of the major characters in relationship to their growth toward becoming truly altruistic in motive as well as in deeds. Overall, she perceives Hardy's efforts as being successful in creating an interesting and effective novel. Her observations are interesting but could be more fully developed.

Mistichelli, William. "Androgyny, Survival, and Fulfillment in Thomas Hardy's *Far from the Madding Crowd.*" *Modern Language Studies* 28.3 (1988): 53-64.

The focus of Mistichelli's article is the character Bathsheba Everdene and an interpretation of her sexuality as presented in the novel. He views Bathsheba as being somewhat androgynous since she possesses traits that are both typically male as well as those that are typically female. Using examples from the text to support his claims, he says:

> The relevance of sexual mixing and reversal is at the center of the novel's action and theme. Androgyny in its various manifestations colors the conflicts which arise among the major characters and contributes significantly to their resolution. (54)

Mistichelli describes Bathsheba's relationships with Oak, Troy, and Boldwood and discusses their perceptions of her character traits. He provides a series of examples from the text that serve both to illustrate the complex nature of Bathsheba's character and to show the ways in which the three suitors approach their relationships with her.

Mistichelli concludes by saying, "the movement of the novel points to the ultimate fulfillment of the heroine within her marriage to the proper mate" (62). He also reminds readers that Bathsheba initiates the marriage proposal and as a result a certain sense of equality between the two is achieved. In general, this article is well organized and provides a sufficient amount of detail to lend credence to Mistichelli's observations.

Shires, Linda M. "Narrative, Gender, and Power in *Far from the Madding Crowd.*" *The Sense of Sex.* Ed. Margaret R. Higonnet. Chicago: University of Illinois Press, 1993. 49-65.

Shires argues against feminist criticism that simply reverses the opinions expressed by males who reviewed Hardy's work during the Victorian period (50). She states:

> While preceding feminist readings align power with the male victimization with the female . . . I argue for Hardy's representations of gender as subtle, mobile, and heterogeneous. (51)

She explores the relationship between gender and power throughout the text of *Far from the Madding Crowd.* She separates the narrative into several sections and begins with a discussion of Gabriel Oak's power as it relates to his masculinity. Somewhat later she discusses the issue of power and femininity as seen in Bathsheba Everdene. Shires looks specifically at two scenes in the novel where she argues that Hardy is exploring the essence of women. One of the scenes cited by Shires occurs when Bathsheba has the opportunity to view Fanny's corpse. The second scene identified by Shires is that following the viewing when Bathsheba runs to the swamp for refuge. Shires explains that when confronting the body of the woman whom Troy states he loves, Bathsheba seeks to gain the power that belongs to Fanny by dying herself. She concludes by arguing that while the novel's ending in some sense realigns "cultural constructions of gender and biology" (64), this occurs only after a radical destabilizing of power in earlier portions of the text. Although the article is somewhat difficult to follow, the issues raised by Shires merit close examination. She successfully argues her case and provides readers with unique insights.

Swann, Charles. "*Far from the Madding Crowd*: How Good a Shepherd is Gabriel Oak?" *Notes and Queries* 39.2 (1992): 17.

Swann evaluates the authenticity and effectiveness of Gabriel Oak's practices as a sheep farmer. After consulting with at least two modern sheep farmers, Swann comes to the conclusion that Hardy's information related to the practice of raising and caring for sheep properly was, at best, faulty. He explains that it is doubtful that a sheep farmer would allow his dogs to eat a dead sheep. He also states that it is highly unlikely that a successful sheep farmer would leave an inexperienced dog out at night as Oak does in the novel. Swann's observations are persuasive and his points well taken.

Wittenberg, Judith Bryant. "Angles of Vision and Questions of Gender in *Far from the Madding Crowd*." *The Centennial Review* 30.1 (1986): 25-40.

Wittenberg begins by discussing the role visual perception or sight plays in *Far from the Madding Crowd*. She says that this novel "represents a culmination of his [Hardy's] treatment of the various visual preoccupations that are evident in all the work of his early period" (26). She goes on to describe the vantage points from which the male characters view Bathsheba and how the sight of her affects their sexual desires. Wittenberg observes:

> That Hardy was far more candid in his treatment of sexual matters than his Victorian contemporaries has long been acknowledged; by examining Hardy's depiction of the male gaze, we can see that candor was of an extraordinary range. (28)

Also discussed is the gaze of the public and its subsequent judgment of the actions of the various characters. The perceptions of each of the principal characters are described and references are made to the blending of both feminine and masculine attitudes within such characters as Bathsheba and Oak. The article is clearly written and seems to make observations that are not overstated but which provide insight regarding the roles of the principal characters.

Weir on the Frome (Froom) near West Stafford: "Only one sound rose above this din of weather, and that was the roaring of a ten-hatch weir a few yards further on, where the road approached the river which formed the boundary of the heath" (Book Fourth, Chapter IX, *The Return of the Native*).

Chapter IV
The Return of the Native

Circumstances of Composition

There is still some dispute about the actual dates of composition of *The Return of the Native*. Sources generally agree that the novel was largely composed during Hardy's stay at Riverside Villa in Sturminster Newton. However, little is known regarding the precise time Hardy began to develop his conception of the novel or when he began to write the initial draft. Studies by R. L. Purdy and Michael Millgate reveal that it is likely that Hardy began work on the novel sometime in 1876, since by February of 1877, Hardy had mentioned to a friend that he had sent a portion of the manuscript to Leslie Stephen, editor of the *Cornhill* magazine (Millgate 187). Although both the *Cornhill* and *Blackwood's Magazine* rejected the novel for serial publication, it was finally accepted for publication in *Belgravia*. The first installment was published in January of 1878 (Purdy 27).

There are a number of other unusual circumstances relating to the composition and publication of this particular novel. In his somewhat dated work, John Paterson argues for the existence of an UR-novel (8). He states:

> The existence of the UR-novel is first of all betrayed by an irregularity in the physical structure of the manuscript. (8)

Then, Paterson goes on to describe various aspects of the text that indicate that it was greatly altered throughout the composition process. He discusses the naming and renaming of the major characters, such as Eustacia, formerly Avice, and Wildeve, formerly Toogood (8). Paterson also describes in some detail Eustacia's evolution from a thoroughly sinister witch to a more romantic, and less sinister, heroine (16-19).

Another unusual circumstance associated with the novel's publication is Hardy's apparent interest in the illustrations that would accompany the text. Both Purdy and Millgate describe Hardy's dissatisfaction with Arthur Hopkins's initial illustration of Eustacia Vye (Purdy 25, Millgate 197). There is also evidence to suggest that Hardy offered suggestions to Hopkins regarding the way Eustacia should look. Purdy records that Hardy told Hopkins that Eustacia should have been presented as younger looking and softer in appearance (26). This would seem to lend support to Paterson's views relating to Hardy's move toward the creation of a more likable, less wicked heroine. Nevertheless, just how much of Paterson's theory can be accepted is still open to question.

In addition to discussing the composition process and publication details, it is important to discuss the early critical reception of the novel as it was, in general, less favorable than Hardy had received for such novels as *A Pair of Blue Eyes* and *Far from the Madding Crowd*. In her article "The Reception of Thomas Hardy's *The Return of the Native*," Joan Pinck examines a series of critical responses to the novel as published by Smith and Elder in 1878. She argues that while the reviewers found certain aspects of the novel praiseworthy, they also found much to condemn. In referring to the early reviews, Pinck states that they

> represent instances of the critic's taking away with one hand what he had given with the other; with this novel Hardy both pleased and displeased his critics most of the time. (293)

Current critical work seems to be somewhat similar in its evaluation of the novel, although in general critics have come to recognize more fully the strength of Hardy's portrayal of the character of Eustacia Vye.

One final area of particular interest is the setting. It appears significant that Hardy included a map of the setting in the first edition of the story. In his article titled "Topography in *The Return of the Native*," J. Hillis Miller devotes a great deal of discussion to Hardy's creation of Egdon Heath. He goes so far as to say that

> The personification of the heath is the covert manifestation of the ubiquitous presence of the narrator's consciousness. . . . The characters in the novel are, insofar as they are embodiments of the heath, therefore also indirectly representatives of the narrator. (126)

Within Miller's article is a reproduction of the map drawn by Hardy as well as a segment of an actual ordnance survey map dated at about the time Hardy had been working on the novel. Much praise has been given to Hardy's creation of the Heath and numerous photographs of the supposed area have been printed. It may seem redundant to emphasize the beauty present in Hardy's description of the landscape in *The Return of the Native*, but his detailed discussions of the features of the Heath stand out as one of his crowning achievements as a writer.

Works Cited

Miller, J. Hillis. "Topography in *The Return of the Native.*" *Essays in Literature* 8.2 (1981): 119-134.

Millgate, Michael. *Thomas Hardy: A Biography*. New York: Oxford University Press, 1985.

Paterson, John. *The Making of "The Return of the Native."* Westport, CT: Greenwood Press, 1978.

Pinck, Joan B. "The Reception of Thomas Hardy's *The Return of the Native.*" *Harvard Library Bulletin* 17.3 (1969): 291-308.

Purdy, Richard L. *Thomas Hardy: A Bibliographical Study*. Oxford: Clarendon Press, 1968.

Davis, William A. "Clough's 'Amours De Voyage' and Hardy's *The Return of the Native*: A Probable Source." *English Language Notes* 31.1 (1993): 47-55.
Davis turns to the poem "Amours De Voyage" by Arthur Hugh Clough as a possible source of inspiration for Hardy. Based on notes taken by Hardy prior to and during the composition of *The Return of the Native*, Davis feels that it is highly probable that Hardy had been reading Clough's poem. He says, "This reading, I believe, provided the raw material for Hardy's study of discontent, escape and return in *The Return of the Native*" (48-49). Davis draws parallels between and among Claude, Clym, Eustace, and Eustacia. He cites specific examples from the text of the poem and the text of the novel. Davis also stresses

the importance of recognizing the themes that are common to both works. His insights are intriguing and clearly presented.

Gatrell, Simon, ed. *The Thomas Hardy Archive: 2* (A Facsimile of the Manuscript with Related Materials). New York: Garland, 1986.

This particular selection is, simply put, extremely arresting to examine. The reproduction of the manuscript renders the material, in general, clear enough to read throughout the handwritten text. The various additions, deletions, and corrections made by Hardy can be seen in the manuscript. The introduction written by Gatrell helps guide the reader through the manuscript and provides a discussion of particularly significant features in Hardy's text. Information regarding the circumstances surrounding the novel's publication is also provided, as is Hardy's map of the setting as he envisioned it.

Millgate, Michael. *Thomas Hardy: A Biography.* New York: Oxford University Press, 1985.

Chapters 9 and 10 in Millgate's book are of special interest to readers of *The Return of the Native.* Here, Millgate discusses the composition process of the work and describes the circumstances surrounding its initial publication. Also included in the chapters is information about Hardy's relationship with his first wife, Emma. It is interesting to note that while living at Sturminster Newton, the location where most of the manuscript was composed, Hardy and Emma described this as being their "happiest time" together. Millgate also presents information regarding the critical reception of the novel and Hardy's anxious reaction to it. In addition, he points out autobiographical elements within the text.

Paterson, John. *The Making of "The Return of the Native."* Westport, Connecticut: Greenwood Press, 1978.

Although some of Paterson's ideas have since been challenged, much of the material he presents is still useful to readers of *The Return of the Native.* Chapter 2, where he begins to describe the presence of an UR-novel, is of special interest. Paterson gives examples from the manuscript of various names Hardy had contemplated using instead of Eustacia, Clym, and Johnny, and describes some changes made by Hardy involving the relationships between and among the principal characters. Also mentioned is the addition of the sixth book at the end of the novel. This is significant because a different ending to the novel seems to have been planned by Hardy, and many have argued that the wedding between Thomasin and Diggory Venn is not consistent with the tone of the novel. Perhaps the most significant aspect of the UR-version discussed by Paterson is the development of the character Eustacia Vye. He provides evidence from the manuscript which shows that as originally conceived, Eustacia was a much more sinister heroine. Although Paterson argues that it is not known if editorial concerns were the reason behind the significant changes made in Eustacia's character, the changes merit examination because Eustacia, as she appears in the final version, is both a powerful and an engaging presence. It should, however, be noted that many current critics' conclusions differ from Paterson's on the basis of further investigations.

Pinck, Joan B. "The Reception of Thomas Hardy's *The Return of the Native*." *Harvard Library Bulletin* 17.3 (1969): 291-308.

Pinck primarily examines the reviews of Hardy's *The Return of the Native* that appeared in the year 1878, just after the novel's publication in book form. She provides numerous examples and compares the remarks of the various reviewers. Pinck also offers information about the tastes of the Victorian reading audience and identifies some of the differences between the criticism of the Victorian period and more recent critical trends. In referring to the overall critical response to the novel, she states, "Clearly the consensus of the reviews of *The Return* is unfavorable, despite the praise with which the criticism is larded" (308). The article is well organized, and the information presented by Pinck helps readers to better understand the audience for which Hardy was writing.

Purdy, Richard L. *Thomas Hardy: A Bibliographical Study*. Oxford: Clarendon Press, 1954.

Purdy gives detailed information regarding the publication history of the novel *The Return of the Native*. He describes the condition of the manuscript and provides information about the composition of the novel. The information is presented in an organized and succinct fashion. Information specific to *The Return of the Native* can be found on pages 24-27. Descriptions of both the serial version and the three-volume hardbound edition are included. This work by Purdy is helpful to both the general reader and the scholar.

Comparative Studies

Benway, Ann M. Baribault. "Oedipus Abroad: Hardy's Clym Yeobright and Lawrence's Paul Morel." *The Thomas Hardy Yearbook* 13 (1986): 51-57.

Benway begins by comparing Clym Yeobright to Oedipus. She states "Hardy's novel has a closer relationship to Sophocles' play than does Lawrence's, but *Sons and Lovers* fits more nearly the Oedipal myth as it has been abstracted by psychologists" (51-52). Benway then describes the similarities between Mrs. Yeobright and Mrs. Morel and their respective relationships with their sons. Later, she examines the depth of Clym's relationship with Eustacia and draws comparisons to that between Paul and Clara. Although the article is brief, it is informative and the comparisons noted by Benway are worth examining.

Evans, Robert. "The Other Eustacia." *Novel* 1.3 (1968): 251-259.

Evans argues that while a first reading of *The Return of the Native* may leave readers with the sense that Eustacia Vye is a tragic heroine, additional readings may reveal "a selfish and self-deceiving girl, incapable of assuming responsibility, to whom love is but an intense and short-lived physical experience . . ." (251). He continues his argument by describing Eustacia as she is first seen in the novel and makes specific references to the language used to describe her. In the second portion of the article, Evans looks at the patterns of behavior associated with Eustacia. He examines her responses to Clym's questions about her love for him and asserts that Eustacia's actions and words are similar to those expressed by many adolescents. Further, he argues that, "Like so many others who entertain romantic misconceptions of the world, Eustacia has little warmth and spontaneous good feeling for others" (255). Evans concludes the article by explaining that Hardy was unable to join successfully the two aspects of Eustacia's character, and so he finds a weakness in the novel that he is unable to excuse.

Magee, John. "Hardy's *The Return of the Native*." *The Explicator* 53.4 (1995): 216-217.

In this brief selection, Magee refers to Hardy's narrator's borrowing of "an epigram from Joseph Addison's *Cato* to foreshadow the consequences of hesitation" (216). He describes the actions of the principal characters but places emphasis on the fate of Damon Wildeve. He argues that it is Wildeve's inability to make a decision without hesitation that leads eventually to the loss of his life and perhaps even his soul.

Mickelson, Anne Z. "The Family Trap in *The Return of the Native.*"
    Colby Library Quarterly 10.8 (1974): 463-475.

The primary subject of investigation in Mickelson's article is the Yeobright family, specifically Mrs. Yeobright and Clym. She notes that Hardy's presentation of Mrs. Yeobright is as "one of those strong women denied self fulfillment by society and forced to seek it through the men in her family" (466). Mickelson then describes the type of relationship that exists between Mrs. Yeobright and her son Clym. Further, she compares this relationship to that of Mrs. Morel and Paul in D. H. Lawrence's *Sons and Lovers*. In addition, Mickelson compares Clym to Merseault (*The Stranger*), Billy Pilgrim (*Slaughter-House Five*), Rasselas (*The History of Rasselas: Prince of Abyssinia*), and others. Also addressed by Mickelson is Hardy's use of imagery. Although some of her points are worthy of consideration, her ideas could be more fully developed.

Ray, Martin. "Hardy's Borrowing from Shakespeare: Eustacia Vye and
    Lady Macbeth." *The Thomas Hardy Yearbook* 14 (1987): 64.

In this short selection, Ray suggests that perhaps Hardy came to regard "Eustacia as a kind of Lady Macbeth figure in the later stages of his novel" (64). He refers specifically to a scene in chapter 4 of the novel, in which Eustacia is presumably thinking of using one of her grandfather's pistols to commit suicide. Ray links this scene to Scene I, Act V of *Macbeth*, where Lady Macbeth is denied access to any weapons because it is feared that she will take her own life. The language used in both works supports Ray's assertions. His observations have merit, and this brief article is informative.

Vandiver, Edward P. "*The Return of the Native* and Shakespeare."
    Furman Studies 12.1 (1964): 11-15.

The focus of this brief article is the relationship between *King Lear* and *The Return of the Native*. Also mentioned as possible sources of influence are *Othello* and *Hamlet*. The scene described in greatest detail by Vandiver is the scene when Mrs. Yeobright visits Clym after his marriage to Eustacia. He likens the relationship between Lear and Cordelia to that which exists between Mrs. Yeobright and Clym.

Nature of the Novel

Gadek, Lois Groner. "Tragic Potential and Narrative Perspective in Hardy's *The Return of the Native*." *The Thomas Hardy Yearbook* 14 (1987): 25-35.

Gadek addresses two major features of *The Return of the Native* in terms of its overall tone. She looks at two contrasting views of humanity as presented in the novel, as well as two distinct narrative approaches used throughout the work. In addition, Gadek examines Hardy's use of allusion in the classical sense and refers to his attempt at creating a novel which would observe the unities of time, place, and action (25). Gadek presents background information regarding the publication history of the novel suggesting that the novel developed over a period of time and was subject to numerous revisions. She stresses that Hardy's original plan was eventually altered, noting that "when the editor of *Belgravia* and some of Hardy's readers objected to the sad ending of the story, Hardy wrote a sixth book" (26). She goes on to point out that by adding a sixth book, Hardy caused a breakdown in the structure of the novel. Gadek states that "This addition ruined the analogy to the five-act structure associated with Greek tragedy and also destroyed the proposed unity of time" (26). However, in the remaining portion of the article, she describes how the setting and the narrator's view of humanity permit a tragic interpretation of the novel. When discussing the narrative technique, Gadek argues that there are two approaches taken by the narrator when setting the scene or describing a character: one view is distant and critical while the other is close and sympathetic. Further, she would assert that the narrative technique helps to illustrate the two contrasting views of man:

> The broader, impersonal perspective Hardy cultivates throughout the book provides a total background out of which the observations about man's insignificance organically grow. (34)

However, when the narrator uses the closer, more sympathetic perspective, it is possible for the reader to "respond to the predicaments and conflicts of the characters" (34). This, in turn, creates a sense that individuals are important and unique.

Jagdish, Chandra Dave. *The Human Predicament in Hardy's Novels*. London: Macmillan, 1985.

In Part II of Jagdish's study of Hardy's novels is a section devoted to *The Return of the Native*. He allocates nearly 30 pages to the discussion of this novel, beginning with a description and analysis of the setting. Lengthy examples from the text are included, followed by brief comments on symbolism and theme. Somewhat later, Jagdish examines the attributes of the characters Eustacia Vye and Clym Yeobright. He describes Eustacia's attitude as being one of revolt and Clym's as one of resignation. Also examined is the attitude of Mrs. Yeobright toward the marriage of Thomasin and Damon Wildeve, as well as Clym's marriage to Eustacia. In addition, Clym's reaction to the death of his mother and the sense of responsibility he feels for her death as well as Eustacia's is discussed. In general, this section is well organized and not overly difficult to read (although other sections are more complicated) and may prove helpful to those interested in more general discussion of the novel.

Meisel, Perry. *Thomas Hardy: The Return of the Repressed*. New Haven, CT: Yale University Press, 1972.

Chapter 3 in Meisel's book is specifically devoted to a discussion of *The Return of the Native*. He begins this chapter by describing some of Hardy's thoughts as they were expressed in notes written near the time the novel was conceived. Meisel argues that Hardy was consciously developing his ideas about how and what to write, and that *The Return of the Native* marked a transitional phase for Hardy. He makes the point that

> The importance of *The Native* lies in its discovery that the source of the community's potential for downfall lies within the deep recesses of the nature of society itself. (89)

The actions of the characters Clym Yeobright and Eustacia Vye are discussed at length, as is the significance of Egdon Heath as the landscape against which the action takes place. The tension between Clym's and Eustacia's ambitions is also explored. The chapter is somewhat difficult to read in isolation, but the information presented here is useful to students of the novel.

Trezise, Simon. "Ways of Learning in *The Return of the Native.*" *The Thomas Hardy Journal* 7.2 (1991): 56-65.

Trezise's approach to the issue of education as found in *The Return of the Native* is unique and intriguing. He argues that "the evolution of Clym's ideas on education form a constant theme in the novel" (58). To support this assertion, he provides background information on the time period in which the novel is set, along with an explanation of various aspects of the Chartist Movement. In discussing Clym in particular, Trezise states:

> Clym Yeobright in *The Return of the Native* is Hardy's contribution to a traditional debate on the role of education which was itself part of a larger debate on the condition of England. (57)

Interspersed throughout the article are numerous examples from the text that provide insight regarding Clym's views on education. Also included are various references to different ways of reading and writing. Trezise says, "The text constantly evokes the metaphor of reading and writing as the way of understanding people and the natural environment" (61). This is an interesting observation when viewed alongside Clym's philosophy of education. Trezise concludes by arguing that in spite of Clym's efforts to provide the residents of the heath with a more modern view of education, he is unsuccessful in securing the happiness and fulfillment that he believes education can provide.

Salient Features of the Novel

Atkinson, F. G. "The Inevitable Movement Onward—Some Aspects of *The Return of the Native.*" *The Thomas Hardy Yearbook* 3 (1972): 10-17.

Atkinson discusses the significance of time as it relates to the sequence of events that occurs in *The Return of the Native*. He argues that although Hardy may have worked to preserve the unity of place within the novel, he did not strictly observe the unity of time. Atkinson further asserts that the sixth section of the novel, titled "Aftercourses," is an essential part of the novel and "that *The Return of the Native*, though revised by its author more often and more radically than any of his other novels, was arranged in six books from its earliest inception" (17). Here, it is important to note that the series of events described in "Aftercourses" occur outside of the year and one day framework. Throughout the article, Atkinson challenges the arguments made by Joseph Warren Beach in *The Technique of Thomas Hardy*. While Beach would argue that the organization of *The Return of the Native* indicates Hardy's attempt to adhere to the principles of dramatic unity, Atkinson maintains that the organization of the novel as it appeared in serial and book form weakens Beach's arguments. The assertions made by Atkinson are interesting, but a more thorough investigation into the circumstances of composition and publication of *The Return of the Native* would have made the challenge to Beach's assertions more compelling. A prior reading of *The Technique of Thomas Hardy* would prove helpful to readers of Atkinson's book.

Bjork, Lennart A. " 'Visible Essences' as Thematic Structure in Hardy's *The Return of the Native.*" *English Studies* 53 (1972): 52-63.

The basic premise of Bjork's evaluation seems to be valid, but some portions of the article are difficult to follow. He argues that

> The description of Egdon Heath, then, establishes the thematic frame of reference: the antithesis between life in Ancient Greece and that in nineteenth-century England. (54-55)

He goes on to assert that identifying and understanding this major theme is essential to understanding the characters Clym Yeobright and Eustacia Vye. He discusses each character in relation to the aforementioned theme and cites numerous, though brief, examples from the text to support his claims.

Corballis, Dr. Richard. "A Note on Mumming in *The Return of the Native.*" *The Thomas Hardy Yearbook* 5 (1975): 55-56.

Dr. Corballis identifies and describes the practice of mumming as presented in *The Return of the Native*. Corballis refers specifically to a dice game played by Diggory Venn and Damon Wildeve. He also provides information regarding the etymology of the term *mumming* and relates the derivations in meaning to the characterization of Diggory Venn. Corballis states that "the characterization of Diggory Venn was strongly influenced by Hardy's knowledge both of mumming and of nineteenth-century thinking on the etymology of the word" (56). Corballis presents his ideas in a succinct and effective manner.

Grinsell, Leslie. "Rainbarrows and Thomas Hardy." *The Thomas Hardy Journal* 2.2 (1986): 59-61.

Grinsell describes the possible origins of the term *Rainbarrow* and its appearance in the novel *The Return of the Native*. Grinsell points out that while "The earlier editions of *The Return of the Native* before 1895 call the focal point of the novel Blackbarrow throughout" (60), later editions have been altered and use *Rainbarrow*. Also included in the article is a brief discussion regarding the practice of opening barrows for the purpose of obtaining artifacts. The information presented in the article is interesting and may help readers to understand more about the unique topographical features described in the novel.

Hawkins, Desmond. "The Birds of Egdon Heath." *The Thomas Hardy Journal* 7.3 (1991): 86-87.

In this brief article, Hawkins discusses the appearance of various types of birds in *The Return of the Native*. He specifically examines the descriptions given by the narrator at the beginning of chapter 10. He says, "Hardy opens chapter 10 with a sketch of Egdon's bird-life which is designed to strengthen the general impression of the Heath's apartness and abnormality" (86). Hawkins goes on to point out that Hardy's knowledge about birds most probably comes from his research rather than personal observation, and, therefore, to examine his sources of reference "is to gain an added insight into the way Hardy selected and adapted his material" (86).

Jewell, John. "Hardy's *The Return of the Native*." *The Explicator* 49.3 (1991): 159-162.

This article presents information on Hardy's use of color in *The Return of the Native*. Jewell specifically addresses the significance of the color red and its association with the character Diggory Venn. Jewell provides readers with background information on the use of reddle and says that in the novel "reddle functions as a kind of scarlet letter" (160). Further, Jewell argues that "Diggory Venn signals for Hardy's readers the presence of illicit love and passion" (160). To support his claims, Jewell provides several examples from the text. However, he concludes the article by reminding readers that by the end of the novel Diggory is no longer involved in the reddle trade. This, Jewell argues, is "the one seeming inconsistency in Venn's function in the novel" (161). Overall, the observations made by Jewell help to provide insight into the character Diggory Venn and help readers to better understand the significance of the color red as it is used throughout the novel.

Miller, J. Hillis. "Topography in *The Return of the Native*." *Essays in Literature* 8.2 (1981): 119-134.
Miller's interesting and somewhat complicated discussion centers on Hardy's creation of Egdon Heath. The basis for Miller's discussion of the Heath is his belief that

> A novel may be thought of as figuratively a mapping in the sense that the story traces out diachronically the movement of the characters from house to house and from time to time, as the crisscross of their relationships gradually creates a mental or imaginary space. (120)

The particular space Miller examines is, as mentioned, the setting of *The Return of the Native*. Included in the article is a map of Dorchester as it was in 1873 and a map drawn by Hardy representing the scene of the novel. Also discussed by Miller is the personification of the Heath. He provides a series of extensive examples from the text to support his assertions and states his arguments clearly and skillfully.

Smith, J. B. " 'Bees up Flues' and 'Chips in Porridge': Two Proverbial Sayings in Thomas Hardy's *The Return of the Native*." *Proverbium* 12 (1995): 315-322.
Smith examines two expressions found in *The Return of the Native*. Specifically, he discusses the origin of the expression "Bees up Flues" and "Chips in Porridge." He views Hardy's use of such phrases as an extension of the dialect used by many of the characters in the novel and explains their significance within the context of the text. Smith also presents information regarding the usage of dialect throughout various regions in England and compares a variety of expressions that have essentially the same meaning.

Squillace, Robert. "Hardy's Mummers." *Nineteenth-Century Literature* 41.2 (1986): 172-189.
Squillace provides an explanation of the significance of the mummers' play as depicted in *The Return of the Native*. He traces the origins of this type of play but disagrees with critics who assert that Hardy knew of the plays' pagan origins and incorporated it into the novel to evoke related images. Squillace points out that the information

regarding the ancient origins of the mummers' plays was not known or available at the time of the novel's composition. He says:

> That Hardy says nothing in the novel itself to connect mumming with primitive rituals may be the strongest evidence that he did not know there was any such connection. (177)

Squillace identifies the mummers' play as a vehicle used by Hardy to reinforce the theme of identity that is present throughout the novel. In laying the foundations for his arguments, Squillace provides readers with an abundance of interesting and well-documented information.

Wyatt, Bryant N. "Poetic Justice in *The Return of the Native*." *Mark Twain Journal* 21.4 (1983): 56-57.

Wyatt addresses the system of justice as represented in the novel. He argues that the actions of the characters are not evaluated in conventional terms but rather on the basis of their conformity to the society of the Heath. Although some interesting observations are made by Wyatt, the brevity of the article limits the strength of his arguments.

Character Analysis

Cohen, Sandy. "Blind Clym, UnChristian and Christian and the Redness of the Reddleman: Character Correspondences in Hardy's *The Return of the Native*." *The Thomas Hardy Yearbook* 11 (1984): 49-55.

This article is devoted to the discussion of three specific characters: Clym Yeobright, Christian Cantle, and Diggory Venn. Cohen argues that Hardy's "Familiarity with Latin, Greek, German and French literature" (49) as well as his "familiarity with the Scriptures" (49) influenced the creation of the characters presented in Hardy's novels. Cohen links Clym to Oedipus, Diggory Venn to Christ, and Christian Cantle to Hermes. The article is divided into four sections. Each character is discussed individually, and numerous specific examples from the text of *The Return of the Native* are provided. The final section of the article where Cohen attempts to summarize her conclusions is a bit brief. The overall effectiveness of her arguments would have been greatly increased by a more fully developed concluding section.

Grimsditch, Herbert B. *Character and Environment in the Novels of Thomas Hardy*. New York: Russell and Russell, 1962.

Although Grimsditch's discussion encompasses a variety of Hardy's novels, a certain portion of his work is devoted to *The Return of the Native*. The section of particular interest to readers of *The Return of the Native* is section II, titled "Landscape, and Country Life in General." Within this section, Grimsditch allocates nearly ten pages to an examination of Egdon Heath and Eustacia Vye. The significance of the Heath is discussed, as is Eustacia's relationship to it. Also mentioned are Clym Yeobright, Diggory Venn, Damon Wildeve, Thomasin Yeobright, and Mrs. Yeobright. Even though this source is somewhat outdated, the information provided by Grimsditch is helpful in providing readers with a general overview of the work's significance as well as its distinguishing features.

Hyman, Virginia R. *Ethical Perspective in the Novels of Thomas Hardy*. New York: Kennikat Press, 1975.

Hyman's treatment of *The Return of the Native* focuses on the two central characters, Eustacia Vye and Clym Yeobright. She devotes a chapter to each character. Chapter 7 is titled "Eustacia Vye the Romantic Egotist," and chapter 8 is titled "The Evolution of Clym Yeobright." Hyman argues that in *The Return of the Native* Hardy goes beyond his previous works in developing the characters of the novel. She stresses the significance of Hardy's placing Eustacia within a definite historical context where she is isolated in her views from the other characters in the novel. Hyman states:

> From the beginning, Hardy makes Eustacia an anomaly in the present, not only by revealing her exalted notions about herself and about destiny, but socially as well. (61)

She concludes the chapter by discussing the similarities between Eustacia and Clym. The following chapter begins with a discussion of their differences. Hyman views Clym as a "more advanced altruist" (65). Throughout the chapter, Hyman continues to point out the similarities and differences between Clym and Eustacia. She examines such things as their educational background and upbringing. Hyman also makes references to Clym's and Eustacia's views about life. In addition, she discusses Hardy's concerns as a writer about the effects produced by the characters he had created. It is important to note that in chapter 9, titled "Historical Perspective: The Minor Characters,"

Hyman continues her discussion of *The Return of the Native* by exploring the significance and development of minor characters such as Diggory Venn and Mrs. Yeobright. When read in conjunction with one another, the three chapters from Hyman's book provide much insight regarding the characters presented in the novel.

Jordan, Mary Ellen. "Thomas Hardy's *Return of the Native*: Clym
  Yeobright and Melancholia." *American Imago* 39.2 (1982): 101-118.
  Jordan devotes nearly the first half of the article to a discussion of Clym's state of mind. She discusses Clym's disillusionment with Paris and his return to Egdon Heath. In addition, she describes his relationship with his mother and his decision to become a schoolmaster. However, Jordon places primary emphasis upon the structure of Clym's character and his tendency to regard life as something one must tolerate. She says:

> Clym's views are tied to a long series of losses, which led him first to disillusion, then to depression, and finally to the melancholia which develops upon the deaths of his mother and wife. (103)

In order to explain further Clym's sense of loss, Jordan turns the discussion to Eustacia. Jordan points out Eustacia's tendency to be depressed like Clym. She also describes the similarities in the traits of Eustacia and Mrs. Yeobright as a possible explanation for Clym's attraction to the former. She concludes her discussion by examining the sixth book of the novel and says that here Clym's "heroic potential deteriorates into melancholia" (118). Jordan provides a series of examples from the text, and although her arguments are interesting they are presented in a somewhat disjointed manner.

Larson, Dixie Lee. "Eustacia Vye's Drowning: Defiance vs.
  Convention." *The Thomas Hardy Journal* 9.3 (1993): 55-63.
  Larson examines Eustacia's death in relationship to a "nineteenth-century stereotype, the motif of the drowned woman" (55). She describes Eustacia's behavior in the novel as being outside that which was expected of the Victorian female and refers to Mrs. Yeobright's perceptions of her as being dangerous to Clym. Larson states, "Eustacia's failure to conform to society's idealized view of womanhood is most evident in her insistence upon passionate love" (57). However, Larson also argues that after the break in her relationship with Clym, Eustacia experiences a change in her attitudes

and behaviors. She feels that this change in Eustacia was created by Hardy so that her suicide would make sense within the context of the story and Eustacia's development as a character. Larson's arguments are convincing and well stated, and although not all readers interpret Eustacia's death as suicide, Larson's observations merit careful inspection.

May, Charles E. "The Magic of Metaphor in *The Return of the Native*." *The Colby Library Quarterly* 22.2 (1986): 111-118.

In his article, May focuses on the character Eustacia Vye. May asserts that Eustacia functions as an *archetype* as well as a *real person*, and in doing so can be examined on both psychological levels. To support his claims he refers to the works of various psychological theorists and provides a variety of examples from the text. Although the article is brief, May is able to establish his arguments as credible and to guide readers through a somewhat complicated interpretation of the novel.

Zellefrow, Ken. "*The Return of the Native*: Hardy's Map and Eustacia's Suicide." *Nineteenth-Century Fiction* 28.2 (1973): 214-221.

Zellefrow attempts to convince readers of *The Return of the Native* that Eustacia's death was most definitely a suicide. In arguing his case, Zellefrow points to specific passages in the text that he feels serve to illustrate Eustacia's suicidal tendencies. In addition, he points to the numerous revisions made by Hardy as evidence that Hardy "wished to establish her death as the result of conscious choice" (219). Although Zellefrow's premise is interesting, the article is short and does not seem to present enough evidence to support his argument.

The King's Arms Hotel, Dorchester, Dorset: "The building before whose doors they had pitched their music-stands was the chief hotel in Casterbridge, namely the King's Arms. A spacious bow-window projected into the street over the main portico" (Chapter V, *The Mayor of Casterbridge*).

Chapter V
The Mayor of Casterbridge

Circumstances of Composition

The writing of *The Mayor of Casterbridge* coincided with Hardy's return to Dorchester and the building of his final home, Max Gate (Easingwood 64). The significance of Hardy's move to Dorchester from Wimborne is explained by Michael Millgate, who states, "Hardy had returned to Dorchester precisely in order to be in closer touch with all the traditions, customs and values of his family and his region" (*Biography* 247). This is important to note because the setting of the novel, the fictional city of Casterbridge, bears a strong resemblance to the Dorchester of the mid-1800's. Millgate also points to Casterbridge "as the social, economic, and geographical center of an entire Wessex world" (248). In establishing Casterbridge as the center of *Wessex*, Hardy had more clearly defined the borders of this fictional region.

Although Hardy seems to have been more at ease in his writings when he was in the familiar surroundings of his childhood home, he still appears to have had doubts about the direction his work should take. Numerous critics describe the extensive revisions of the text of *The Mayor of Casterbridge* as evidence of Hardy's concern about the nature of his writing in the artistic sense as well as the nature of his writing in an economic sense. In referring to novel writing as a trade, Peter Easingwood succinctly states, "Hardy's success made him susceptible to pressure from sources in the trade claiming to represent popular opinion" (65). This, as stated earlier, seems to have affected the composition process of *The Mayor of Casterbridge*.

In the article "The Manuscript of Hardy's *The Mayor of Casterbridge*," Christine Winfield describes a number of the changes made by Hardy as found in the manuscript. Several of the principal changes are also described by Michael Millgate in his book *Thomas Hardy: His Career as a Novelist*. The revisions identified by Winfield and Millgate involve not only revisions of the plot but also changes in the characteristics and relationships of the central characters. Winfield remarks that

> Henchard and his wife were originally conceived as older than they appear in the present text. They had been married for five years, with one daughter at least old enough to offer her mother advice. (47).

Additional evidence suggests that the details of Henchard's relationship to Lucetta underwent several changes, even after the novel's initial publication in serial form. Winfield observes that "the sexual element in the relationship—remained suppressed until the publication of the first uniform edition of 1895" (57).

While examination of the existing manuscript has yielded a variety of interesting details, the examination of possible sources of inspiration for Hardy has also proved enlightening. Numerous critics and scholars describe Hardy's voracious reading habits as well as his habit of taking extensive notes. Millgate describes Hardy's systematic reading of the Dorset County Chronicle and the incorporation of material found there into the narrative of *The Mayor of Casterbridge* (*Biography* 248). He, as does Michael Taft, refers to local and to regional records of wife-selling incidents as directly linked to the opening events described in the novel (*Biography* 248). Another source of inspiration for Hardy, as alluded to earlier, was the city of Dorchester itself, and although even today various locations in Dorchester strikingly resemble specific places associated with Casterbridge, Millgate argues that Hardy's primary concern was "not so much to enumerate the town's visual features—topographical, architectural, archaeological—as to evoke the precise texture of its social and economic life" (*Career as a Novelist* 222). This being said, one can still derive a great amount of pleasure from visiting Dorchester and identifying what seem to be recognizable features of the Casterbridge Hardy created in the novel.

After the novel's initial publication in the *Graphic* in 1886, and the novel version published in the same year, the reviews were mixed. Some praised Hardy's creation of Henchard while others puzzled over Hardy's choice of subject matter. Today, however, there seems to be a more general type of agreement regarding the strength of Hardy's portrayal of Henchard as well as a recognition of the significance of

Henchard's struggles. In a relatively recent article, Ronald Draper describes Henchard's role in the novel:

> Henchard is the dominant character; no other figure in the novel approaches him in stature, and no other receives the same amount of attention (57)

Essentially, as stated by Draper and as implied by the subtitle of the work ("The Life and Death of a Man of Character"), the story is about Michael Henchard's rise and fall. Although many critics have taken the time to describe in some detail the actions and characteristics of various other characters in the novel, the most significant impression left with the reader is that created by the central character, the Mayor of Casterbridge, Michael Henchard.

Works Cited

Draper, Ronald P. "*The Mayor of Casterbridge.*" *Critical Quarterly* 25.1 (1983): 57-70.

Easingwood, Peter. "*The Mayor of Casterbridge* and the Irony of Literary Production." *The Thomas Hardy Journal* 9.3 (1993): 64-75.

Millgate, Michael. *Thomas Hardy: A Biography.* New York: Random House, 1982.

— — —. *Thomas Hardy: His Career as a Novelist.* New York: St. Martin's Press, 1994.

Taft, Michael. "Hardy's Manipulation of Folklore and Literary Imagination: The Case of the Wife-Sale in *The Mayor of Casterbridge.*" *Studies in the Novel* 13.4 (1981): 399-407.

Winfield, Christine. "The Manuscript of Hardy's *Mayor of Casterbridge.*" *The Papers of the Bibliographical Society of America* 67 (1973): 33-58.

Caless, Bryn. "The Nomenclature of Hardy's Novels: *The Mayor of Casterbridge.*" *The Thomas Hardy Yearbook* 5 (1975): 96-98.

In this short selection, Caless examines the various names assigned to the characters Michael Henchard and Donald Farfrae throughout the composition process. Caless discusses the origins of the names and offers possible explanations for Hardy's revisions of them. Caless says that before settling on the name Michael, this character was first called Giles and then James. Caless also discusses the possible origins of the surname Henchard, and further suggests that each of the names Hardy selected provides insights into the final development of the character:

> When Hardy abandoned the name "James" in favor of "Michael", it is probably because he wanted to marry the two ideas of "limitation" and "nobility" in the man—these forces for good and evil which are counterbalances in his character.

Caless concludes the article by examining the Scottish origins of Farfrae and describing Hardy's reasons for adopting the name Donald Farfrae for the character he had called Alan Stansby. Caless's observations are interesting, but they seem somewhat speculative in nature.

Easingwood, Peter. "*The Mayor of Casterbridge* and the Irony of Literary Production." *The Thomas Hardy Journal* 9.3 (1993): 64-75.

Easingwood discusses the composition of *The Mayor of Casterbridge* as it coincides with the building of Max Gate. He describes Hardy's social position at the time of writing, as well as the demands placed on authors who published their works in serial form. Easingwood views *The Mayor of Casterbridge* as a work that carries on a *double-discourse*. He says that "the story is designed to meet the demands of the market for fiction but the text also pens itself as a more open work to readers" (65). Easingwood also devotes a fair amount of discussion to the expectations of the Victorian reading audience as well as to Hardy's departure from previously established formats. In addition, he examines the development of *Wessex* and points out features within Hardy's landscape that reveal "that Wessex is not the culturally homogeneous setting it may superficially be mistaken to be" (69). Since this article is relatively current, and since Easingwood discusses the novel as a whole while also providing some background information on Hardy, this article proves to be especially helpful and informative.

Greenslade, William. "Hardy's 'Facts' Notebook: A Further Source for *The Mayor of Casterbridge*." *The Thomas Hardy Journal* 2.1 (1986): 33-34.

Greenslade provides a description of notes taken by Hardy around the time he was writing *The Mayor of Casterbridge*. He discusses several newspaper accounts read by Hardy that are closely related to events and locations described in the novel. Greenslade states that scenes in the early part of the novel were "suggested to Hardy by a report of the decline in trade at Weyhill Fair near Andover in the late 1820's" (33). Although this article is very brief, it provides interesting information regarding Hardy's source(s) of inspiration.

Raine, Craig. "Conscious Artistry in *The Mayor of Casterbridge*." *New Perspectives on Thomas Hardy*. Ed. Charles P. C. Pettit. New York: St. Martin's Press, 1994. 156-171.

Although complicated and somewhat difficult to follow, Raine's article does help readers better understand Hardy's technique as a writer. Raine begins by describing the critical responses of Henry James and G. K. Chesterton to Hardy's works, and he takes issue with their dismissal of Hardy's talents. Further, Raine goes on to explain how certain scenes in *The Mayor of Casterbridge* serve to illustrate Hardy's control over his narrative. He argues that Hardy's talent

> is for simplicity, an apparent simplicity, a "delicate imposition" which is actually intensely sophisticated both in its strategic grasp of structural necessity and its cunning local tactics. (159)

To support his assertions, Raine examines the characters Michael Henchard and Donald Farfrae. He specifically addresses the way Hardy presents Henchard in the final chapters of the novel. Raine describes the incidents surrounding Henchard's eventual death and Hardy's treatment of them. He continually refers to Hardy's choice to avoid the direct description of significant events by allowing one of the minor characters to describe the given situation in great detail. In general, Raine seems to have been successful in his attempt to identify and describe some of the more interesting aspects of Hardy's writing.

Winfield, Christine. "The Manuscript of Hardy's *Mayor of Casterbridge*." *The Papers of the Bibliographical Society of America* 67 (1973): 33-58.

In her examination of the manuscript of *The Mayor of Casterbridge*, Winfield primarily focuses on the types of revisions that appear throughout the text. She discusses the development of the text and asserts that three stages of development can be identified. Winfield describes the type of paper and ink used by Hardy and explains the types of markings that helped her identify the chronological layers of the manuscript. She states:

> Evidence that Hardy subjected his work to revision immediately after and sometimes during the act of composition (or perhaps more accurately, during the act of copying) is provided by the canceled material on the verso of a number of sheets which contain the discarded beginnings of several leaves. (39)

To further illustrate the extent of Hardy's revisions, Winfield examines the naming and renaming of Donald Farfrae. She also examines the changes in relationships among the principal characters, as well as various alterations made within the plot. Many examples from the text are provided and Winfield's discussion is sufficiently detailed as to provide readers with a great deal of information regarding the composition of the novel.

Comparative Studies

Aschkenasy, Nehama. "Biblical Substructures in the Tragic Form: Hardy, *The Mayor of Casterbridge* and Agnon, *And the Crooked Shall Be Made Straight*." *Modern Language Studies* 13.1 (1983): 101-110.

Aschkenasy opens the article by discussing the similarities between the two novels: *The Mayor of Casterbridge* and *And the Crooked Shall Be Made Straight*. The observation is made that

> the two works call our attention to the sometimes mysterious ways in which folk motifs and literary patterns travel across countries and cultures and find themselves in different settings. (101)

Like many other critics, Aschkenasy refers to Hardy's allusion to the story of King Saul and David. The characteristics of Henchard and Farfrae are compared with those of King Saul and David, as is the development of their respective relationships with each other. Later, Aschkenasy refers to Oedipus Rex as another source of inspiration for Hardy. In referring to Henchard, Aschkenasy says, "Hardy, then, draws the image of the diseased monarch from both Hebraic and Hellenic sources" (104). The discussion of Hardy's novel is followed by an examination of *And the Crooked Shall Be Made Straight* by Agnon. Aschkenasy draws comparisons between Hardy's Henchard and Agnon's Menashe-Hayim. At the close of the article, it is noted that "while the Biblical presence functions as a supportive substructure in both works, the two writers differ in their use of the Biblical material" (108). Although certain aspects of Aschkenasy's arguments are thoroughly explained, a knowledge of both works under discussion is essential for a complete understanding of the article.

Cooley, John R. "The Importance of Things Past: An Archetypal Reading of *The Mayor of Casterbridge.*" *Massachusetts Studies in English* 1 (1967): 17-21.

Cooley describes the relationship of *The Mayor of Casterbridge* to a number of narrative selections. He likens elements in the plot to the stories of Oedipus, Hamlet, and King Saul. Cooley says:

> The reason so many close parallels exist between the Henchard-Farfrae plot line and earlier literature is because Hardy touched upon one of the archetypal patterns which appears endlessly in legend and myth. (20)

He also finds parallels in the characteristics of Michael Henchard and King Saul as well as Donald Farfrae and King David. Although many of the observations made by Cooley are intriguing, his arguments could be more fully developed.

Dollar, Gerard D. "Addiction and the 'Other Self' in Three Late Victorian Novels." *Beyond the Pleasure Dome: Writing and Addiction From the Romantics*. Ed. Tim Armstrong et al. Sheffield, England: Sheffield Academic Press, 1994. 268-274.

In his examination of the novels *The Strange Case of Dr. Jekyll and Mr. Hyde* (Stevenson), *The Mayor of Casterbridge* (Hardy), and *Picture of Dorian Gray* (Wilde), Dollar focuses on two themes present throughout each of the works. His interest is in the duality of man's nature and "the fascination with—combined with a horror of—addiction" (268). Dollar deals primarily with the central character in each of the novels. He compares the actions of Dr. Jekyll, Michael Henchard, and Dorian Gray. In discussing their various addictions, he states:

> The initial, heady feeling of liberation achieved by Dr. Jekyll, Michael Henchard and Dorian Gray leads only to another worse enslavement: the substance which appeared to be the key to unlocking a more powerful and appealing inner self ends up as the jailer. (273)

To support his assertions, Dollar provides examples from each of the texts and links them together with concise explanations. His approach is unique and his arguments are clearly presented.

Egan, Joseph T. "The Indebtedness of George Douglas Brown to *The Mayor of Casterbridge.*" *Studies in Scottish Literature* 27 (1992): 203-217.

The primary subject of Egan's article is the similarity that exists between *The Mayor of Casterbridge* and *The House with the Green Shutters*. Published just more than a decade after Hardy's novel, Brown's work reflects some of the same themes as Hardy's. Yet, Egan asserts that "the strongest link between the two is found in the character and destiny of their protagonists . . ." (204). He describes the social status of each character and identifies traits that are shared by Michael Henchard and John Gourlay. Egan also discusses the plot of each novel in some detail. He provides numerous examples from each text and is successful in arguing that the relationship between the novels was a result of something more than chance.

Humma, John B. "*Sister Carrie* and Thomas Hardy, Regained." *Dreiser Studies* 23.1 (1992): 8-26.

Humma begins by describing a brief passage originally cut by Dreiser at the initial printing of *Sister Carrie*. The passage contained a conversation among several of the principal characters and was reprinted in a later edition of the text. Various literary works are being discussed by the characters, and Carrie mentioned that she had read *The Mayor of Casterbridge*. Humma views this scene as necessary and feels that by its removal, essential insights into Carrie's development are lost. Further, he argues that the scene served to indicate the influence of Hardy on Dreiser. Humma says that Dreiser's reading of Hardy "influenced not only the tone and spirit of the novel but also character and plot" (12). Later, Humma compares specific sections of Hardy's work to Dreiser's. Near the close of the article, he draws numerous connections between *The Mayor of Casterbridge* (as well as *Tess of the d'Urbervilles*) and *Sister Carrie*. The article is well written and Humma's arguments are convincing.

Nature of the Novel

Bair, Judith. "*The Mayor of Casterbridge*: 'Some Grand Feat of Stagery.' " *South Atlantic Bulletin* 42.2 (1977): 11-22.

Bair disagrees with critics who view the story of *The Mayor of Casterbridge* as a tragedy. Instead, she argues that "Hardy diminishes the tragic stature of Henchard and his story by his consistent application of the motif of the stage" (11). She goes on to describe the structure of the narrative and to examine a variety of scenes from the novel. Bair refers to Susan and Elizabeth-Jane's first observation of Casterbridge and states "the image of Casterbridge as a stage is richly developed, as we come to learn that it is constructed on layers of dramatic platforms" (14). She describes Henchard's actions as being those of a performer and notes his failure to fulfill his role or to maintain his act. To support her assertions, Bair examines Henchard's behavior in detail. She describes the various roles played by Henchard as mayor, businessman, husband, and father. In general, her approach is interesting and her examination of the stage motif provides insight into elements within the novel. However, her conclusions about the status of Henchard can still be challenged.

Davis, Karen. "A Deaf Ear to Essence: Music and Hardy's *The Mayor of Casterbridge*." *Journal of English and German Philology* 89.2 (1990): 181-201.

Davis's discussion is somewhat complicated and abstract, yet her emphasis on the two musical theme groups that run throughout the novel is intriguing. She asserts that there is a rivalry between two groups of tones, those that roar and are dynamic and those that are quieter and more lyrical. Davis also discusses the presence and absence of sounds as presented in the narrative. She states:

> It is through such interweaving of sounds and silences, momentums and pauses, aggressive repetitions and lyrical interventions that Hardy establishes at the outset the two contrasted theme groups of *The Mayor of Casterbridge*. (183)

In the remaining portion of the article, Davis cites numerous examples from the text to illustrate Hardy's repeated use of musical terminology. She describes Henchard's actions in great detail and refers often to the scene of the skimmity-ride. In addition, Davis draws attention to the significance of the roles of the minor characters.

Draper, Ronald P. *"The Mayor of Casterbridge." Critical Quarterly* 25.1 (1983): 57-70.

Draper describes *The Mayor of Casterbridge* as tragic in the Aristotelian sense as well as the Schopenhauerian. He spends a great deal of time describing the actions of Michael Henchard and the readers' reaction to his rise and fall, and goes on to assert "that the personal fate of Henchard is only a part—even if the most prominent part—of a tragic vision which is expressed in the novel's entire complex of time, place, and character" (62). Next, Draper describes various features of the town of Casterbridge. He notes the significance of the three inns: The King's Arms, The Three Mariners, and the inn owned by Peter Finger. Later, Draper discusses the aspect of time and its relationship to the inhabitants of Casterbridge. He concludes by restating his belief that the novel reflects both Aristotle's and Schopenhauer's views of tragedy and argues that "the result is a novel which is all the greater for being so oddly at variance with itself" (69). The article provides readers with an interesting discussion of the novel, and the references to the views of Aristotle and Schopenhauer are presented in such a way as to render Draper's arguments clear to the general reader. Also, since the views of Schopenhauer are often referred to in Hardy criticism, an article such as this helps readers to better understand not only the novel, but also other critical interpretations.

Haig, Stirling. " 'By the Rivers of Babylon': Water and Exile in *The Mayor of Casterbridge." The Thomas Hardy Yearbook* 11 (1984): 55-62.

Haig examines two devices used by Hardy throughout *The Mayor of Casterbridge*. He begins by describing water as being associated with decline. He refers to Henchard's drunkenness, his problem with the wet grain, and his contemplation of suicide while standing near a deep pool. Next, Haig discusses the ways in which the main characters (as well as some of the minor) are alienated from the society of Casterbridge. He says, "The most obvious and numerous allusions to foreignness cluster about the personage of Lucetta" (59). However, he also describes the foreignness of Henchard, Farfrae, Susan, and Elizabeth-Jane. Haig points out that in the case of each character, their individual link with

Casterbridge is thin. Although a bit brief, Haig's article is engaging and informative.

Kiely, Robert. "Vision and Viewpoint in *The Mayor of Casterbridge*." *Nineteenth-Century Fiction* 23.2 (1968): 189-200.

Kiely begins his discussion of the novel by examining Hardy's use of differing narrative perspectives to provide readers with insights regarding specific characters and events. He explains that by sometimes maintaining "authorial omniscience" and sometimes allowing a character or group of characters to provide narration, Hardy is able to present readers with a variety of perspectives from which to interpret the text. Kiely also feels that the vantage point from which the characters view themselves as well as others is significant. He argues that "The way people look at themselves and one another is the central concern of the novel. What each character sees defines, to a great extent, what he is" (190). Next, Kiely examines Henchard's view of himself. He describes several scenes where Henchard's motives are misinterpreted by other characters, and he notes the severity of Henchard's judgment of himself. In addition, Kiely examines the characteristics of Farfrae, Elizabeth-Jane, and Lucetta that lend a unique slant to their way of viewing the situations in which they find themselves. In closing the article, Kiely refers to Henchard's desire, as expressed in his will, to be out of the view of the other principal characters. He explains how Henchard's inability to gain a proper perspective results in his alienation from himself as well as from others. The points made by Kiely are clearly expressed and his insights serve to guide readers in a more thorough study of the novel.

Salient Features of the Novel

Bebbington, Brian. "Folksong and Dance in *The Mayor of Casterbridge*." *English Dance and Song* 40 (1978): 111-115.

In this brief selection, Bebbington explores the attitude of the Casterbridge community toward Michael Henchard and Donald Farfrae. Bebbington argues that Donald's ability to sing as well as dance helps him become a part of the community or an active member of the social group. He points out that while Henchard can appreciate music, he cannot join the group in song and does not join them in dance. Bebbington argues that Hardy uses the "integrative aspect of folksong and dance, that is, their potential for changing a person's status from individual to member of a group" (115) to make the acceptance of Farfrae and the rejection of Henchard credible.

Chapman, Raymond. "The Reader as Listener: Dialect and Relationships in *The Mayor of Casterbridge*." *The Pragmatics of Style*. Ed. Leo Hickey. London: Routledge, 1989. 159-178.

The first portion of the chapter devoted to a discussion of *The Mayor of Casterbridge* deals with the nature of dialogue itself. Chapman describes the nature of spoken language and the effects it produces within the context of a rural setting. Then, he describes the nature of dialogue within the text of a novel. He distinguishes between the use of dialect and the use of the received standard. Chapman also identifies some of the conventions employed by authors to convey the use of a particular dialect without causing confusion for the reader. Here, he turns his discussion to Hardy's use of dialect and says:

> His [Hardy's] awareness of dialect was well used in the service of his best qualities as a novelist: his sensitivity to both social and personal relationships, and his capacity for conveying the feelings of his characters towards each other. (170)

In his discussion of *The Mayor of Casterbridge*, Chapman provides a number of extensive examples from the text and describes the effects produced by the exchange of dialogue within each excerpt. He looks at how dialect can be used to reveal a character's sense of isolation, social status, emotional state, or function within the novel. Although somewhat complicated, Chapman's discussion addresses in detail a feature of Hardy's writing that has been the cause of much dispute in Hardy criticism. His approach points out the importance of such discussion and helps readers in their examination of Hardy's works.

Epstein, Leonara. "Sale and Sacrament: The Wife Auction in *The Mayor of Casterbridge*." *English Language Notes* 24.4 (1987): 50-57.

Epstein focuses her discussion on the sale of Susan to Newson by Henchard. She argues that "the sale that severs the alliance between Mr. and Mrs. Michael Henchard is also a wedding that creates a union between Mr. and Mrs. Richard Newson" (50). Epstein goes on to describe Victorian views regarding marriage and Hardy's handling of such views within the text. Later, Henchard's second marriage to Susan is described. The relationship between the church wedding and the sale that occurred at the carnival is examined in some detail. The authenticity of each of the *ceremonies* is examined, as are Henchard's motives during each of the events.

Fussell, D. H. "The Maladroit Delay: The Changing Times in Hardy's *The Mayor of Casterbridge.*" *Critical Quarterly* 21.3 (1979): 17-29.

Fussell opens his discussion of *The Mayor of Casterbridge* with a quote from the novel *Tess of the d'Urbervilles.* He briefly examines the similarities between the two novels in terms of the theme of change. He describes *The Mayor of Casterbridge* as being a novel about families and what happens to them as a result of time and circumstance. Fussell goes on to identify changes that take place in the lives and personalities of several of the principal characters. Somewhat later in the article, he discusses the relationship between money and class affiliation. Here Fussell explores both Henchard's and Elizabeth-Jane's reactions to the various changes that occur in their financial status throughout the novel. He identifies and describes some of the actions taken by each of the two characters and says that "what Hardy suggests continuously throughout the novel is that past actions survive like buildings to form obstacles in the present which must be negotiated" (25). Russell devotes the remainder of his discussion to the influence of time and/or timing on the lives of Michael Henchard, Susan, Lucetta, Elizabeth-Jane, and Donald Farfrae. He draws general conclusions regarding Hardy's novels and the impressions with which they leave readers. Overall, the article itself provides readers with information relating to significant themes in *The Mayor of Casterbridge*, and Fussell includes interesting and helpful comments regarding Hardy's achievement in his writing as a whole.

Higbie, Robert. "The Flight of the Swallow in *The Mayor of Casterbridge.*" *English Language Notes* 16.4 (1979): 311-312.

In this short selection, Higbie discusses the significance of the scene early in the novel where a swallow flies into the tent where Susan is sold by Henchard. He cites an earlier work by Bede that seems to offer a similar sentiment regarding the transitory nature of life. He also mentions the small caged bird that found death outside Elizabeth-Jane's door at the end of the novel. He compares Henchard first to the swallow that flies freely through the tent and then the caged bird that dies a solitary death. In addition, Higbie links the movement of the events in the novel to the flight imagery.

Ingersoll, Earl G. "Troping and the Machine in Thomas Hardy's *The Mayor of Casterbridge.*" *University of Hartford Studies in Literature* 22.2-3 (1996): 59-67.

Ingersoll begins the article with a somewhat complicated discussion of the interpretation of various literary terms. He goes on to point out the significance of the use of two terms in particular, metaphor and metonymy, in relationship to their use in *The Mayor of Casterbridge*. Ingersoll views the use of metaphor in association with Henchard and the ways of the past while connecting the use of metonymy with Farfrae and technological development. He also discusses the relationship of Henchard and Farfrae to Elizabeth-Jane and Lucetta. Although several interesting points are made by Ingersoll, his arguments are somewhat difficult to follow and may present some obstacles for the general reader.

Moses, Michael Valdez. "Agon in the Marketplace: *The Mayor of Casterbridge* as Bourgeois Tragedy." *The South Atlantic Quarterly* 87.2 (1988): 219-251.

Although the introductory paragraphs in Moses's article may seem somewhat daunting to the general reader, the remaining portion of this lengthy piece is well organized and not difficult to read. Moses discusses in detail his evaluation of *The Mayor of Casterbridge* as a bourgeois tragedy. He devotes a great deal of attention to addressing the similarities between the city of Casterbridge and that of an ancient city or *polis*. Moses states:

> By suggesting that Casterbridge is a modern bourgeois variant of the *polis*, I wish to argue that Hardy sought out political conditions in a contemporary world which would make possible a rebirth of traditional tragedy. (223)

Following this discussion, Moses explains that while there are many similarities between Casterbridge and the traditional *polis*, there are also a number of significant differences. The differing nature of politics as practiced in an ancient city and that practiced in Casterbridge is specifically addressed. Later, Moses examines certain aspects of Michael Henchard's rise and fall within the Casterbridge community. He goes on to examine the influence of change upon Henchard's status as caused by the arrival of Farfrae, Elizabeth-Jane, and Lucetta. Near the end of the article, Moses identifies two specific strands in the plot, one that involves Henchard's public life and one that centers on his private life. Ultimately, Moses concludes that *The Mayor of Casterbridge* cannot be described as a tragedy in the traditional sense, but he does not seem to dismiss the quality of Hardy's works. He simply states that "In short, Hardy ran up against the limitations placed upon a would-be-tragic writer by the changed conditions of the modern world" (248). In general, Moses aids readers in their understanding of an ongoing discussion of the nature of *The Mayor of Casterbridge* as a tragic novel.

Taft, Michael. "Hardy's Manipulation of Folklore and Literary Imagination: The Case of the Wife-Sale in *The Mayor of Casterbridge.*" *Studies in the Novel* 13.4 (1981): 399-407.

Taft identifies and describes several possible sources of inspiration for the wife-sale in *The Mayor of Casterbridge*. He points out that a number of newspaper accounts of incidents similar to that experienced by the characters Michael and Susan Henchard do exist. Taft also notes that one such account can be found recorded in Hardy's *Facts Notebook*. In addition to the newspaper accounts, of which Hardy must have been aware, Taft cites Hardy's knowledge of popular ballads that incorporate material similar to the newspaper accounts. He includes within the article the text of a ballad that he believes directly inspired Hardy's creation of the wife-sale incident in the novel. Nevertheless, Taft is careful to point out that while the sources of Hardy's inspiration may be identifiable, Hardy's skill in handling the material should be recognized. This particular article provides readers with a brief and informative discussion of one of the principal scenes in the novel.

Character Analysis

Cox, Stevens G. "Giles Symonds Alias *The Mayor of Casterbridge.*" *The Thomas Hardy Yearbook* 3 (1972-73): 24-26.

Cox identifies Giles Symonds as the *original* of Michael Henchard from *The Mayor of Casterbridge*. He discusses various aspects of the man, Symonds, and the character, Henchard. To support his claims, he refers to remarks made by Hardy as well as to a newspaper article describing a particular film adaptation of the novel. Also included in the article is a portion of the obituary notice printed upon the death of Giles Symonds. In addition, Cox notes that manuscript evidence suggests that Hardy had at one time planned to use the name Giles rather than Michael for the central character in the novel. To those interested in identifying possible *originals* for Hardy's characters, this article provides pertinent information.

Gatrell, Simon. *Thomas Hardy and the Proper Study of Mankind.* Charlottesville: University Press of Virginia, 1993.

Gatrell begins chapter 5, titled *"The Mayor of Casterbridge*: The Fate of Michael Henchard's Character," by discussing the various titles Hardy gave to the novel and exploring its emphasis on Henchard's position as mayor. He also examines Henchard's need for power and his need to love. Gatrell feels that these needs are in opposition to one another because of the circumstances that arise within the plot. In other words, if Henchard had not become so attached to Farfrae, his desire for power may not have run contrary to his desire for love. Gatrell goes on to explore how Henchard moves from pouring out his affection on Farfrae to becoming attached first to Elizabeth-Jane and then to Lucetta. Later, after he has been rejected by the three objects of his affection, Henchard turns to drink. Gatrell asserts that Henchard's craving for power does not subside until he wrestles Farfrae and nearly kills him. He states, "The episode has finally buried Henchard's desire for power, and he finally ceases to be mayor" (73). Later, Henchard again desires the companionship of Elizabeth-Jane, but the return of her father, Newson, prevents Henchard from maintaining their relationship. Near the end of the chapter, Gatrell discusses the nature of the narrator's views on Casterbridge. In addition, parallels between Henchard's character and Eustacia Vye's character are drawn. This particular chapter in Gatrell's book provides readers with a solid overview of the novel, while it also helps readers in their examination of some of the salient features in Hardy's fiction.

Giordano, Frank R., Jr. *"I'd Have My Life Unbe"*: *Thomas Hardy's Self-Destructive Characters.* Tuscaloosa, Alabama: University of Alabama Press, 1984.

The focus of chapter 5 in Giordano's study of Thomas Hardy's characters is on Michael Henchard. Giordano asserts that Hardy's representation of Henchard renders him as powerful as characters like

Tess (*Tess of the d'Urbervilles*) and Eustacia (*The Return of the Native*). He states:

> Michael Henchard seizes command of the novel in the opening chapter at the furmity tent, and with his virility, aggressive energy, and ambivalent passions dominates the book until he dies. (78)

Throughout the chapter, Giordano examines the types of relationships that Henchard develops with the other characters in the novel. He first describes Henchard's relationship with Susan at the beginning of the novel, and then discusses Henchard's behavior toward her at various moments within the text. Later, Giordano describes how Henchard becomes involved with Donald Farfrae, Elizabeth-Jane, and Lucetta. In addition, he examines the depth of Henchard's passionate nature as well as the influence of chance upon the circumstances of Henchard's rise and fall. Giordano also discusses Henchard's violation of the established social code. He describes the struggles faced by Henchard in psychological and sociological terms. In general, the chapter is organized as a chronological discussion of the novel and serves as a guide to broad discussion of its distinguishing features as well as Henchard's development as the central character.

Grimsditch, Herbert B. *Character and Environment in the Novels of Thomas Hardy*. 1925. New York: Russell and Russell, 1962.
This book essentially examines the *Wessex* novels. There are numerous references to *The Mayor of Casterbridge* throughout the work which compare and contrast the various characters from each of the Wessex novels. These characters are also examined in view of the environment, which Grimsditch sees as a destined and powerful force in their development. Throughout the work he relies on certain portions of the novel *The Mayor of Casterbridge* to support his overall assertions regarding this group of novels. The work provides a detailed discussion involving several novels and is useful because of its focus on the Wessex works.

Grindle, Juliet M. "Compulsion and Choice in *The Mayor of Casterbridge*." *The Novels of Thomas Hardy*. Ed. Anne Smith. New York: Barnes and Noble, 1979. 91-106.
In the section devoted to a discussion of *The Mayor of Casterbridge*, Grindle primarily examines Michael Henchard's quest for power and his belief that power can be used effectively to provide solutions to a

variety of problems. She goes on to describe Henchard's attempts to *dominate* and obligate those with whom he forms relationships. Specifically, Grindle describes Henchard's involvement with Farfrae, Susan, and Elizabeth-Jane. In referring to Henchard's relationship with Elizabeth-Jane, she points out that

> It is one of the most striking features of *The Mayor of Casterbridge* that the central relationship is *not* a sexual one, it is one which defies acceptable labeling altogether. (95)

Here, Grindle describes in more detail the nature of Henchard's involvement with and interest in his step-daughter. Later in the chapter, she addresses various other distinguishing features of the novel. She briefly touches upon a discussion of identity and the lies that are told regarding the identities of the principal characters. Also addressed are the topics of self-mockery and the importance of the arena as it reappears throughout the text. In general, the section addresses a number of interesting facets of the novel and provides readers with insights regarding the roles of the central characters and the relationships that they form with each other.

Ingersoll, Earl. "Writing and Memory in *The Mayor of Casterbridge*." *English Literature in Transition* 33.3 (1990): 299-309.
    In this brief article, Ingersoll specifically discusses the relationship between Michael Henchard and Donald Farfrae. He likens their relationship to that of a father and a son, and he describes their roles as being that of father and speaker (Henchard) and son and writer (Farfrae). Ingersoll draws on the comments of Jacques Derrida in *Dissemination* to further develop his ideas. He states:

> Henchard and Farfrae's conflict reveals two diametrically opposed structures of experience, involving issues of knowing and memory as they relate to the difference between speaking and writing . . . (299)

Throughout the article, Ingersoll points to instances where Henchard relies on speaking and memory rather than on writing. He describes Henchard's method of doing business in contrast to Farfrae's. While Henchard relies on his word in making transactions, Farfrae works with written agreements. The shift in their relationship as a result of their business practices is also discussed. The article is interesting and informative, but some terminology is used that may not be familiar to the general reader.

Kramer, Dale. "Character and the Cycle of Change in *The Mayor of Casterbridge*." *Tennessee Studies in Literature* 16 (1971): 111-120.

Kramer begins the article by discussing Hardy's view of history. He describes Hardy's ideas regarding the cyclical nature of change throughout history and relates this to the events in the novel. Kramer then discusses some of the similarities between the characters Michael Henchard and Donald Farfrae. He states that "Farfrae and Henchard have moral shortcomings of the same type, if in different degrees and manifestations" (115). Kramer continues with a fairly detailed discussion of Farfrae and concludes that the characterization of Farfrae is consistent throughout the novel. Although this selection is brief, interesting and significant points are brought out in Kramer's discussion of the novel. The information is accessible and well organized in its presentation.

Langbaum, Robert. "The Minimization of Sexuality in *The Mayor of Casterbridge*." *The Thomas Hardy Journal* 8.1 (1992): 20-32.

Langbaum's article provides readers with an illuminating examination of the principal characters from the novel. He begins with a discussion of Michael Henchard and describes Henchard's relationships with Susan Henchard-Newson and Donald Farfrae. Langbaum challenges those who would argue that Henchard's sexuality defines his character by frankly claiming that the text does not support such an assertion. He states:

> In Henchard the desire for power replaces sexuality: he seeks to possess completely the people he loves, or is unable to distinguish the pleasure of love from the pleasure of proprietorship. (22)

While Langbaum does not completely dismiss the notion that some element of homoeroticism seems to be present, he does argue that there are other more important facets of Henchard's character. He goes on to describe the differences between Henchard and Farfrae and to explain why Farfrae succeeds where Henchard has failed. In addition, Langbaum describes Elizabeth-Jane's role as an observer throughout the novel. He explains that her sexuality does not interfere with her judgment and therefore she is able to cope effectively with a variety of different situations as they present themselves. Overall, Langbaum's article is clearly organized and not difficult to read.

Lerner, Laurence. *Thomas Hardy's "The Mayor of Casterbridge"*: *Tragedy or Social History?* London: Sussex University Press, 1975.

Lerner's relatively short book is divided into five chapters. The first chapter is devoted to a discussion of the text in which Lerner reviews plot, character development, and language. He also draws attention to the significance of the subtitle ("The Story of a Man of Character") as it relates to Henchard. In the next chapter, Lerner draws comparisons between and among *The Mayor of Casterbridge* and *Laterre* by Zola as well as *Amaryllis at the Fair* by Richard Jefferies. Also mentioned are several of Hardy's other novels. In subsequent chapters, Lerner examines Hardy's view of life and argues that the novels "are statements of man's tragic situation" (38). He goes on to cite the works of Arthur Schopenhauer as a possible source of influence relating to Hardy's own philosophy. In addition to discussing Hardy's philosophical views, Lerner also discusses various social interpretations of Hardy's work. He describes some of the Marxist criticism of *The Mayor of Casterbridge* and describes the development of the principal characters in some detail. Finally, Lerner concludes by emphasizing the uniqueness of Hardy's style as a writer. In general, Lerner's comments are interesting and helpful. Chapter 4 is especially helpful to those interested in social criticism. The brief reading list at the end of the text points readers to works that are often referred to in Hardy criticism, such as reviews of Hardy's novels.

McCullen, J. T., Jr. "Henchard's Sale of Susan in *The Mayor of Casterbridge." English Language Notes* 2.3 (1965): 217-218.

In this extremely short piece, McCullen describes an account of a wife sale that may have made its way into the local folklore during the time in which Hardy lived. He notes that as many as ten or eleven instances of this nature have been recorded by other scholars, but that the particular account that he refers to is different in tone. The account cited by McCullen (recorded by Catherine Milnes Gaskell) involves the sale of a wife by her husband. The wife insists that the husband go through with the sale even though he is apparently having second thoughts about the transaction. The record of the transaction indicates that the wife stated that she was in need of a change.

Moore, Kevin Z. "Death Against Life: Hardy's Mortified and Mortifying 'Man of Character' in *The Mayor of Casterbridge.*" *Ball State University Forum* 24.3 (1983): 13-25.

Moore focuses on the character Michael Henchard and his inability to create successful relationships with others and argues that this is a result of Henchard's lack of eros, or erotic drive. He states that when Henchard commits the act of selling Susan, "he sells off the last dram of his erotic potential to free himself from binding relationships so that he may advance in the world" (13). Moore goes on to discuss how the period between Henchard's initial separation from Susan and his rise to power is significant precisely because so little information is given about such an extended period of time. He argues that this indicates how Henchard's lack of eros prevents him from becoming connected to others in any meaningful way. Further, he asserts that once Henchard's money and power are taken away, he can no longer buy connections to other people and can no longer function in society. Moore concludes his article by discussing Henchard's repeated attempts to annihilate himself and the memory of his existence. He reiterates his argument that the novel *The Mayor of Casterbridge* is quite distinct from Hardy's other narratives and that Henchard is unlike various other heroes or heroines presented in the novels. Although the article is somewhat lengthy and portions of Moore's arguments are difficult to follow, his insights regarding Henchard's character are thought provoking and certainly provide a foundation for much further discussion of the novel.

Schweik, Robert C. "Character and Fate in Hardy's *Mayor of Casterbridge.*" *Nineteenth-Century Fiction* 21 (1966): 249-262.

Schweik describes the existence of four particular movements or cycles that occur throughout *The Mayor of Casterbridge*. He points out that as Henchard repeats the cycle of hope followed by catastrophe, he changes in character and in action. Schweik describes each of the four cycles in detail and provides specific chapter references for each of the cycles. He also discusses Henchard's relationships with Susan, Farfrae, and Elizabeth-Jane. In addition, Schweik identifies attributes in Henchard's character that directly affect his behavior. He states, "what Hardy repeatedly dramatizes is Henchard's frustrated incapacity to find either the will to destroy or the means to win pardon" (257). Schweik goes on to describe how the reader's perception of Henchard changes as the novel progresses. He comments upon to Elizabeth-Jane's ability to cope with what life has offered her and to her recognition that Henchard may have suffered more than he had deserved. In general, the article is logically organized and Schweik's views are clearly stated. His approach to the examination of the text aids readers in their development of a more thorough understanding of Henchard's character as well as of Hardy as a writer.

Sumner, Rosemary. *Thomas Hardy: Psychological Novelist*. New York: St. Martin's Press, 1981.

In chapter 5, titled "Henchard: The Unruly, Volcanic Stuff Beneath the Rind," Sumner examines Hardy's treatment of Henchard in *The Mayor of Casterbridge*. She says, "A close examination of Henchard's nature and the ways in which he changes illustrates Hardy's profound understanding of aggression" (59). She continues her discussion by looking at aspects of Henchard's character and the results of his impulsive, aggressive behavior. Sumner describes Henchard's relationships with Farfrae, Elizabeth-Jane, Susan, and Lucetta. She discusses the various changes that occur in Henchard's mental state. Sumner asserts that

> This remarkable presentation of a personality is so powerful because Hardy succeeds in making the reader involved in the shifting, changing, conflicting mental states of his character. (66)

She examines, as is suggested by the title of her book, the psychological development of Henchard in relationship to previous as well as current psychological theory. Throughout the chapter devoted to the study of Henchard, Sumner also addresses many significant elements within the novel as a whole. The information and analysis presented in this portion of Sumner's work provide readers with a variety of insights regarding Hardy's methods of characterization as well as Henchard's growth within the novel.

Stafford House near West Stafford, Dorset: "It was vegetable nature's own home; a spot to inspire the painter and poet of still life" (Chapter VIII, *The Woodlanders*).

Chapter VI
The Woodlanders

Circumstances of Composition

The initial printing of *The Woodlanders* in serial form in the spring of 1886 was followed by its appearance in book form in March of 1887. As was common practice, the book form of the novel was published just one month prior to the printing of its conclusion in the final installment of the serial version (Purdy 56-57). The various subsequent editions of *The Woodlanders* reflect other interesting aspects of publishing practices during the 1880's, as well as Hardy's reactions to the pressures put upon by his reading audience. In his "Note on the Text" for the World Classics Edition, Hardy scholar Dale Kramer describes the existence of at least ten versions of the novel. In a somewhat earlier article, Kramer describes in greater detail his own findings regarding the evolution of the definitive text (Wessex Edition, 1912). Of the eight editions listed within the article, the first four editions are of special interest.

In discussing Hardy's decision to market his book in England as well as America at the same time, Kramer states:

> The economic necessity for simultaneous publication of *The Woodlanders* is an essential factor in the formation of the unique American texts. Before 1891 there was no copyright protection in the United States for works published in England. (137)

The two American texts referenced here (*Harper's Bazaar*, Harper and Brothers book edition) were each set from a set of proofs different from each other as well as those used for versions of the novel printed in England. Apparently, Hardy was working with three sets of proofs that he revised differently at various stages in the printing process, both at home and abroad, and as is also pointed out by Kramer, it is not known whether the printers at *Harper's Bazaar* or *Macmillan's Magazine* were aware that the alterations made in each set of the aforementioned proof sheets were not identical (Kramer 139). The final point of interest regarding the serial versions of the novel is that specific expressions and/or sentences believed to be offensive to the English reading public were not deleted from the American serial version as printed in *Harper's Bazaar*, "demonstrating a more liberal editorial policy than in England where 'My God!' was replaced in *Macmillan's Magazine* by 'My Heaven!' " (145).

In terms of the composition process relating to the manuscript version of *The Woodlanders*, it appears that Hardy had difficulty completing the novel in a timely fashion as he prepared for the monthly installments. As many sources point out, Hardy had originally conceived of the idea for this story many years earlier. However, Michael Millgate points out that Hardy had put the idea aside for the purpose of writing a different type of novel so as not to have been described as mainly a writer of the pastoral (173). At the time Hardy began writing the novel, he and his first wife had moved into Max Gate, and Hardy was once again living in the country of his youth. Michael Millgate states:

> Hardy said many years later that he liked *The Woodlanders* as a story, more than any of his other novels, and that preference may have been related to its drawing so richly upon memories. (279)

Certainly the setting chosen by Hardy resembled the areas relatively near his newly built home in the county of Dorset.

In a brief article, M. R. Skilling describes the country of *The Woodlanders* in some detail. She also notes that in trying to identify the original of a fictional setting, individuals may encounter some difficulties. In addition, Skilling describes, as does F. B. Pinion, Hardy's changes in his descriptions of particular features for the specific purpose of rendering its exact location open to question. Yet, Skilling observes that

> Although Hardy had earlier been at some pains to disguise his exact locations, he had slowly realized that there could well be some gain by having associations with a specific geographical region. (63)

Included in Pinion's article titled, "The Country and Period of *The Woodlanders*," are several photographs, a sketch map, and a detailed description of the area believed by many critics to have been the area Hardy had in mind when he established the setting of *The Woodlanders*. Pinion argues that whatever changes Hardy may have made throughout the various stages of the novel's composition, "*The Woodlanders* was imagined in the Melbury Osmund-Melbury Bubb area . . ." (49). Dale Kramer points out that there were two stages in Hardy's development of the setting and, as Pinion also asserts, while initially the action was to occur in the Bubb Down Hill area, Hardy later "moved the action several miles eastward and centered it around High Story Hill" (Introduction, xxiii). Whatever Hardy's reasons for moving the setting (about which there is some disagreement among the critics), it seems not to have detracted from Hardy's overall sense of the novel's story. There is even an amusing account of Hardy having ridden his bicycle throughout the countryside in an effort to pinpoint the exact location of the story for his enthusiastic fans. Apparently, Hardy returned home not having found the precise setting, even though a number of his readers had claimed they had found just the place that Hardy had described (Preface to the 1912 edition).

Works Cited

Kramer, Dale. Introduction. *The Woodlanders*. By Thomas Hardy. New York: Oxford University Press, 1985. xi-xxi.

— — —. "Two 'New' Texts of Thomas Hardy's *The Woodlanders*." *Studies in Bibliography* 20 (1967): 135-150.

Millgate, Michael. *Thomas Hardy: A Biography*. New York: Random House, 1982.

Pinion, F. B. "The Country and Period of *The Woodlanders*." *The Thomas Hardy Yearbook* 2 (1971): 46-55.

Purdy, Richard L. *Thomas Hardy: A Bibliographical Study*. Oxford: Clarendon Press, 1968.

Skilling, M. R. "Investigation into the Country of *The Woodlanders*." *The Thomas Hardy Journal* 8.3 (1992): 62-67.

Kramer, Dale. "Two 'New' Texts of Thomas Hardy's *The Woodlanders*." *Studies in Bibliography* 20 (1967): 135-150.

Kramer lists and describes eight known authorized versions of *The Woodlanders* as published in England and/or the United States. The focus of his discussion is on four of the eight versions as the four (the manuscript, *Harper's Bazaar*, Harper and Brothers book, and *Macmillan's Magazine*) relate to the evolution of the definitive text. Kramer identifies the Harper's Bazaar edition and the Harpers book version of the novel as being previously unnoted versions of the text. He also explains how publishing laws (or the lack thereof) made it necessary, economically, for Hardy to publish in America and Britain simultaneously. The remaining portion of the article is divided into five sections that focus on Hardy's revisions of the text of *The Woodlanders* as they relate to the development of two distinct American versions of the novel. There is a considerable amount of discussion devoted to the publishing process, and specific examples of revisions within the various texts are given. The article is very informative and the information provided by Kramer helps readers to better understand the intricacies of the publication process as it was during Hardy's lifetime.

Pinion, F. B. "The Country and Period of *The Woodlanders*." *The Thomas Hardy Yearbook* 2 (1971): 46-55.

Pinion identifies and describes the setting of *The Woodlanders* based upon evidence from the text(s) as well as Hardy's own comments regarding the location and the timing of the major events. Pinion examines the nature of the controversy among scholars regarding the topography as presented in the novel as it corresponds to actual locations in Dorset. In addition, he helps to establish more firmly the time period described in the novel by citing the existence of particular laws governing divorce practice in the years 1857 and 1878. Pinion also includes a sketch map as well as several photographs to assist readers in their understanding of his references to specific areas of the county of Dorset. The article is interesting and informative, and it is important to note that Pinion is recognized for his careful research and attention to detail.

Skilling, M. R. "Investigation into the Country of *The Woodlanders*." *The Thomas Hardy Journal* 8.3 (1992): 62-67.

This article is particularly interesting when read in conjunction with Pinion's article titled "The Country and Period of *The Woodlanders*."

Although Skilling and Pinion apparently disagree about Hardy's motivation in rendering the actual location of Little Hintock as somewhat obscure, Skilling does rely on some of the information in Pinion's article. Skilling also refers to the work of Dale Kramer and to Hardy's own correspondence with Edmond Gosse regarding the exact location of specific areas described in the novel. She also describes the process of her research and identifies specific route numbers and road names that can be found on current survey maps. In addition, Skilling includes a brief description of a walking tour that individuals may take in order to see the sites she describes. Although somewhat difficult to interpret without the presence of photographs or a map, Skilling's article would prove to be very helpful to those who have the opportunity to visit Dorset with map and novel in hand.

Springer, Marlene. *Hardy's Use of Allusion.* Lawrence: University Press of Kansas, 1983.

Springer discusses many of Thomas Hardy's novels. She begins with a discussion of Hardy's style in general and then focuses on specific works in subsequent chapters. After this brief introduction, Springer specifically outlines the types of allusion used by Hardy, and gives several examples of each type. Her examination of the text is thorough and offers many insights regarding the significance of certain passages within the novel. She closes her arguments by re-emphasizing the importance of recognizing the various allusions used by Hardy. She says that

> Hardy drew from many worlds to enlarge his own novelistic universe, making his allusions serve his audience as avenues into his fiction . . . He requires of his readers that they bring to his novels an imaginative effort, that they read as connoisseurs. He directs his allusions to the gourmets, and their good taste is well rewarded: Wessex and its people are made vividly visible. (174)

Comparative Studies

Arkans, Norman. "Hardy's Novel Impression—Pictures." *The Colby Library Quarterly* 22.3 (1986): 153-164.

The purpose of Arkans's article is to show the connection between Hardy's novels and certain aspects of French Impressionist artwork, with special focus on *The Woodlanders*. In the opening portion of the article, Arkans describes the characteristics associated with impressionist paintings and then draws various connections between and among several of Hardy's novels in terms of the impressions created by each of the works. Arkans argues that *Far from the Madding Crowd, The Woodlanders*, and *Tess of the d'Urbervilles* all exhibit "facets of Hardy's impressionism" (157). After providing several examples to support his assertions, he turns to a discussion of *The Woodlanders* in particular by saying:

> Like Hardy's other major novels, *The Woodlanders* depicts the changing nature of human experience. The organic growth and continuous evolution we see exhibited in the natural world lie at the core of the human side, also. (159)

Later, Arkans discusses Grace's development as a character. He concludes by linking the nature of her growth to the nature of the relationship between the scene and the figure in an impressionist painting. He equates the woodland scenes repeatedly described in the novel with the scenes depicted in paintings of the impressionist movement, and he argues that the creation of the forest world was necessary in order for Hardy to convey the impressions associated with Grace's story.

Buckler, William E. "Toward a Poetics of Hardy's Novels: *The Woodlanders*." *Dickens Studies Annual* 14 (1985): 327-336.
Buckler takes a unique approach in his criticism of *The Woodlanders*. He opens with a brief discussion of Hardy's knowledge of the works of Aristotle, Wordsworth, and Arnold. Buckler then explains why Hardy may have had a preference for writing poetry rather than novels. He continues by stating his belief that Hardy, as a poet, was able to "transform the sow's ear of the popular novel into the silk purse of the most organically poetic novel canon in English" (328). Buckler then refers to several of Hardy's own statements regarding the purpose or function of art. He follows these remarks by examining *The Woodlanders* in relationship to Hardy's possible motive for writing a story of this kind. Buckler states that

> *The Woodlanders* is, in part, a testing of natural life against unnatural life—of literary organism against literary convention—and the testing inheres in the language, action, or myth, and architecture of the novel. (329)

Buckler also discusses the significance of the roles of the central characters while paying particular attention to the development of Marty South. In addition, he addresses the role of the narrator and describes the narrator's function. Finally, Buckler discusses the difficulty in classifying *The Woodlanders* using traditional literary terms. He likens the novel to a painting or tapestry and concludes by praising the uniqueness of Hardy's fiction.

Casagrande, Peter J. " 'The Shifted 'Centre of Altruism' in *The Woodlanders*: Thomas Hardy's Third *'Return of the Native.' "* *English Literary History* 38 (1971): 104-125.

Casagrande compares and connects various elements in *Under the Greenwood Tree*, *The Return of the Native*, and *The Woodlanders*. He begins by identifying the similarities that exist between and among the principal characters in each of the three novels. Then, he describes briefly the basic plot of each work and to discuss how the theme of the returning native can be seen throughout the group of novels. He includes several charts to help readers visualize the comparisons he makes. The first chart lists the major characters in each novel and identifies each character by type. The second chart represents the structural makeup of each of the works, and the final chart provides readers with a graphic outline of the relationships that develop among the principal characters as presented in each of the individual novels. Later in the article, Casagrande differentiates between the setting of *The Woodlanders* as distinct from the setting of *The Return of the Native*. He asserts that the Hintock Woodlands and Egdon Heath are very different in terms of what each represents. Casagrande states that in "The woodland is Hardy's symbol of man in society—in the society of organic life" (118). Next, he describes Grace's various journeys into the woodland and discusses the significance of each. Casagrande concludes the article by restating that Hardy's novels *Under the Greenwood Tree*, *The Return of the Native*, and *The Woodlanders* are all stories of return and that they "embody in their very structures the central experience of his life and art—the relationship of the old and the new, of the past and the present" (124). Overall, the article provides readers with a series of interesting comparisons regarding the plot, setting, and theme present in each of the novels. The charts are very helpful and present readers with a unique way of looking at the central elements of the novels individually and as a group.

Fontane, Marilyn Stall. "Hardy's Best Story." *The Thomas Hardy Yearbook* 11 (1984): 37-41.

To support her argument that the theme of *The Woodlanders* reveals and encompasses the themes present in the *Wessex* novels, Fontane essentially draws comparisons among and between Hardy's six major works. She asserts that

> Hardy's novels taken as a whole present a memorial to the beauty and peace (and innocence and ignorance) of the old tradition while showing the impossibility of the continuance of that way of life. (38)

Fontane goes on to describe the principal elements in *The Woodlanders*, such as plot, setting, and character development, that illustrate the theme she has identified as running throughout the novel(s). Later, she discusses the role of the group of rustics and the social order of Great Hintock and Little Hintock. Fontane also describes the actions of several of the characters in some detail, with emphasis on the six major characters (Marty South, Giles Winterborne, Mr. Melbury, Grace Melbury, Edred Fitzpiers, and Felice Charmond). She concludes by reiterating Marty South's words regarding the death of Giles Winterborne in which she expresses her desire to remember him and his vanished way of life.

Higgins, Lesley. " 'Strange Webs of Melancholy': Shelleyan Echoes in *The Woodlanders.*" *Thomas Hardy Annual* 5 (1987): 38-46.

Higgins begins by discussing Hardy's reading of Shelley and points to ideas that may have provided inspiration for Hardy. In referring to the setting of the novel, she states:

> The unity of place which Hardy creates—the woodlands are both picturesque and grotesque, evoked in Shelleyan and Darwinian terms—is complemented by the unity of tone. (40)

Later, Higgins points out additional connections with the ideas of Shelley as found in *Queen Mab*. Specifically discussed is Hardy's concept of the Immanent Will. Also referred to are the poems titled "Alastor," "Adonais," and "The Revolt of Islam." Throughout the remainder of the article, Higgins discusses the major themes in *The Woodlanders* as they echo the philosophies of Shelley. A number of examples from the text of *The Woodlanders* are provided, as are examples from the poems of Shelley and the personal notes of Hardy himself. The ideas presented by Higgins are interesting but some prior knowledge of Shelley's writings is necessary for a complete understanding of the article.

Nature of the Novel

Ball, David. "Tragic Contradiction in Hardy's *The Woodlanders*." *ARIEL: A Review of International English Literature* 18.1 (1987): 17-25.

Ball begins his article with a discussion of the nature of tragedy as compared to that of comedy. He then identifies similarities between Giles Winterborne (*The Woodlanders*) and Gabriel Oak (*Far from the Madding Crowd*), but he does point out that while they have similar traits their destinies are very different. Next, Ball describes a variety of incidents (and devices) that appear in *The Woodlanders* that are tragicomic in nature. Included are a number of examples from the text involving Fitzpiers, Grace, and Melbury. Later, Ball focuses on the ending of the novel, and in referring to the death of Giles and Marty's closing speech, he states that

> This is Giles' valediction, the best sense of his death, the completion of the tragedy. The speech is a contradiction composed of consummation and loss, comic and tragic, dominated by loss. (24)

Finally, Ball describes the tone of the novel and its overall somberness. Although the article is brief and a bit fragmented in its presentation, Ball's observations are interesting and provide readers with unique insights regarding the novel's genre.

Bayley, John. "A Social Comedy? On Re-reading *The Woodlanders*." *Thomas Hardy Annual* 5 (1987): 3-21.

Bayley describes the mixing of various genres throughout *The Woodlanders* and addresses the impressions left by the novel as a result of this mixing. He goes on to assert that Hardy's close association with the group of principal characters may account for some of the conflicting or competing genres. Bayley specifically refers to the passivity of Grace Melbury, Giles Winterborne, and Marty South. He describes Hardy's treatment of Giles Winterborne in particular. Bayley states, "Winterborne is the only rustic in his work who is idealized by Hardy, and who exemplifies in individual form that mixture of modes which characterizes the novel" (8). Near the middle of the article, Bayley discusses the nature of the novel as a social comedy. He describes Melbury, Winterborne, and Grace in terms of their connections with society and their attempts to obtain or maintain a certain social status. He identifies what he feels is a "secret humor" within the novel and describes the work as being more psychological and realistic than some of Hardy's other stories. Throughout the remainder of the article, Bayley draws comparisons between and among *The Woodlanders*, *Tess of the d'Urbervilles*, *Jude the Obscure*, *The Mayor of Casterbridge*, and *Far from the Madding Crowd*. He concludes with a discussion of the tone of *The Woodlanders* and restates his interpretation of the novel as a "comedy of small things" (21).

Irvin, Glenn. "Structure and Tone in *The Woodlanders*." *Thomas Hardy Annual* 2 (1984): 79-90.

Irvin discusses the nature of *The Woodlanders* as a tragicomedy. He states that the novel is "a carefully constructed but subdued story that demonstrates the power of comedy to absorb and contain tragedy" (79). Irvin continues his discussion by describing scenes that he feels best illustrate Hardy's use of comedy. He specifically refers to the scene when Giles gives a party for the purpose of bringing his relationship with Grace into focus more quickly. Irvin also identifies the scene of the auction when Giles continually outbids Grace's father. Later in the article, Irvin centers on a discussion of the tone, which "remains somber and does not reinforce the comic plot structure" (84). To support this assertion, Irvin describes various events that take place in relationship to the effects such events produce upon the major characters. He reminds readers of the fate of Giles Winterborne as well as the reconciliation of Grace and Fitzpiers. In the conclusion of the article, Irvin describes how the structure and tone of the novel work together to reinforce the theme of the old order passing away in favor of the new.

Peck, John. "Hardy's *The Woodlanders*: The Too Transparent Web." *English Literature in Transition* 24.3 (1981): 147-154.

Peck examines various aspects of *The Woodlanders* in an effort to explain why it seems to have been "the least admired, and by far the least discussed" (147) of Hardy's major works. He cites the writings of several critics throughout the article but focuses largely on the ideas presented in Ian Gregor's *The Great Web*. Peck agrees with Gregor when he states that in the novel the "characters interrelate in various ways, none being really alone, so that the slightest movement by one makes the whole web quiver" (147). However, Peck goes on to describe the ways in which the style of Hardy's writing in *The Woodlanders* makes the connections (that create the web) too clearly visible and much less powerful than those drawn in the other major novels. He describes Hardy's writing as being too precise and analytical. Peck also expresses dissatisfaction with Hardy's self-assurance in terms of his language use. In referring to Hardy's technique, Peck states that

> In his finer novels he is never so sure of language. They are full of doubts, his own voice is repeatedly challenged, and the awkwardness of his style enacts the difficulties of comprehension. (153)

Peck's observations are interesting because he describes in some detail various unique aspects of Hardy's writing. In addition, his appreciation of Hardy's awkwardness and the effects it produces is not often articulated in this manner. In other words, many critics seem to find this same awkwardness problematic rather than praiseworthy. Therefore, Peck's approach provides readers with an alternative viewpoint regarding Hardy's writing technique.

Salient Features of the Novel

Baldridge, Cates. "Observation and Domination in Hardy's *The Woodlanders*." *Victorian Literature and Culture* 21 (1993): 193-209.

Baldridge challenges claims by various critics who argue that *The Woodlanders* lacks relevance and specificity when compared to such novels as *The Mayor of Casterbridge* and *Tess of the d'Urbervilles*. Baldridge asserts that within the novel *The Woodlanders* there is "a pervasive orientation toward fundamental purposes and effects of viewing in all its forms" (191). Then Baldridge describes the actions taken by Marty South and Giles Winterborne after they have had the opportunity to survey or view a particular set of circumstances. Specifically, Baldridge refers to Marty's perception of the meaning of the conversation between Mr. Melbury and Mrs. Melbury just prior to Grace's return and to Winterborne's surveillance of the Melbury family just after he returns Grace to her father's home. In referring to Giles's reticence or reluctance to act or move towards a relationship with Grace after he sees her on repeated occasions, Baldridge asserts that "there seems to be—for him—something intrinsic to the act of observation itself which renders the process inimical to the accumulation of power" (195). Conversely, Baldridge argues that Fitzpiers is empowered by his observations of Grace and the other characters. Numerous examples from the text of the novel are included throughout the article, followed by clear descriptions of the different ways of seeing associated with each of the major characters. In general, the article is well organized and provides readers with a wealth of information.

Cramer, Jeffrey S. "The Grotesque in Thomas Hardy's *The Woodlanders.*" *The Thomas Hardy Yearbook* 8 (1978): 25-29.

Cramer begins his article by establishing a working definition of the term *grotesque*. Although he lists three elements that can be associated with the *grotesque*, he argues that only two of the elements are present in *The Woodlanders*. The elements he identifies as being present in the novel are "The unjustified fusion of different realms of being" and "Excess and distortion" (26). To support his claims, Cramer provides numerous examples from the text. He refers specifically to the death of John South as it relates to his unreasonable fear of a tree. He also cites several examples where Hardy uses personification to intensify the various descriptions of the forest. The ideas presented by Cramer are intriguing, but the article is somewhat fragmented in its overall presentation.

Greiff, Louis K. "Symbolic Action in Hardy's *The Woodlanders*: An Application of Burkian Theory." *The Thomas Hardy Yearbook* 14 (1987): 52-62.

Greiff's primary interest is in applying Kenneth Burke's literary theory regarding "poetic strategies" and "symbolic actions" to *The Woodlanders*. His examination continues with a description of the sequences of events surrounding Grace's flight to Giles's hut and her subsequent reconciliation with her husband. He states that

> While Grace's escape into the woods is a practical act on her part—to avoid Fitzpiers—it is likewise a symbolic act on Hardy's part, performed in the context of an overall strategy within *The Woodlanders*. (54)

Greiff continues by referring to Burke's "idea of a dialectical structure as the key to any literary work" (54) and asserts that Hardy's attitudes can be discovered by examining Grace's actions. He describes Grace's return to Fitzpiers in some detail and suggests that her final acceptance of Fitzpiers reveals Hardy's own attitudes towards marriage. Greiff provides a number of examples from the text of the novel as well as Burke's *The Philosophy of Literary Form*. Although the article is brief and somewhat limited in scope, Greiff's discussion is well organized and provides readers with a thought-provoking interpretation of the novel.

Hannaford, Richard. "Ragnarok in Little Hintock: Norse Allusions in *The Woodlanders*." *The Thomas Hardy Yearbook* 6 (1976): 30-33.

Hannaford traces the allusions to Norse mythology as they occur throughout the novel. He mentions the scene early in the novel where Marty South overhears Mr. Melbury speak of Grace's return to Little Hintock. Also mentioned is Marty's return through the darkness and her decision to cut her hair because she believes that she no longer has the chance of being courted by Giles. Hannaford likens Hardy's description of the darkness to the Norse idea of ginnungagap. He states:

> The Norse allusion to a ginnungagap-like darkness reinforces this theme that truth is difficult to determine and that characters will reason wildly regardless. (131)

Frequent references are also made to the Norse gods and goddesses such as Loki, Sif, Hel, and Oden. The idea of universal chaos is stressed as the overall tone of lament. The information presented is interesting but the selection is a bit brief, and some of the ideas could be more fully developed.

Hubbart, Marilyn Stall. "Thomas Hardy's Use of Folk Culture in *The Woodlanders*." *Kentucky Folklore Record* 23 (1977): 17-24.

In the opening of the article, Hubbart explains that while the Wessex novels as a group provide readers with a record of the past, *The Woodlanders* in particular includes imagery that renders Hardy's descriptions of rural life especially vivid. Next, Hubbart discusses how the many references to the aspects of daily living help to make the characters in the novel seem more real. Somewhat later, Hubbart turns to a discussion of the plot. She describes Grace's meeting with Giles at the market, Grace's first meeting with Felice Charmond, and the Christmas party given by Giles. Hubbart goes on to describe Grace's courtship by Fitzpiers and their marriage, separation, and reconciliation. Throughout the paragraphs that serve as short plot summaries, Hubbart interjects bits of information regarding nineteenth-century Folklore. She concludes by stating "The folklife of *The Woodlanders* is not just background for, but symbolic of, the story itself" (22).

Thesing, William B. " 'The Question of Matrimonial Divergence': Distorting Mirrors and Windows in Hardy's *The Woodlanders.*" *The Thomas Hardy Yearbook* 14 (1987): 44-52.
In the opening of the article, Thesing identifies and describes the initial critical reception of *The Woodlanders* as well as more recent critical trends relating to the quality of the novel. He points out that past critics, as well as present, have tended to overlook significant features of the novel. Thesing states that

> In *The Woodlanders* Hardy uses two carefully worked-out patterns of imagery to make a thematic statement about relations between men and women. (45)

To support this assertion, he points to Hardy's use of imagery involving mirrors and windows. Thesing argues that "The imagery of mirrors and windows develops the novel's themes of delusion and immature vision" (45). Later in the article, he describes the ways in which the principal characters (Grace, Giles, Marty, and Edred) view their various circumstances. Finally, Thesing closes the article by suggesting that Marty South seems to be the only character who can discern reality and as such, she becomes the only character to experience some sense of fulfillment.

Character Analysis

Hannaford, Richard. " 'A Forlorn Hope?' Grace Melbury and *The Woodlanders.*" *The Thomas Hardy Yearbook* 10 (1980): 72-76.

Hannaford discusses Grace's development as a character by describing her relationships with Giles Winterborne, Marty South, and Edred Fitzpiers. He begins by summarizing the circumstances of Grace's return to Little Hintock and her rejection of Giles. Hannaford points to Giles's failure to act at moments when Grace would have been most likely to renew their relationship. Next, he discusses Marty's passive acceptance of circumstance upon the death of Giles and Grace's eventual return to Fitzpiers once the sting of Giles's death lessens. Hannaford argues that where Giles and Marty experience failure as a result of their lack of action, Grace and Fitzpiers "at least make the gamble for survival" (76). Included in the article are specific examples from the text that describe Grace's move from a passive young girl to a more thoughtful and assertive woman.

Morrison, Ronald D. "Love and Evolution in Thomas Hardy's *The Woodlanders.*" *Kentucky Philological Review* 6 (1991): 32-37.

The focus of Morrison's discussion is on the characters Marty South, Grace Melbury, Suke Damson, and Felice Charmond. He states that each of the four central female characters "serve to emphasize the ways in which Victorian women are both victims and predators in the struggle" (32) for survival. Morrison refers to Hardy's interest in evolution and the works of Darwin as being related to some of the main themes in *The Woodlanders*, but he does go on to say that "Early in the novel, Hardy transfers his focus from the struggle for survival to the human struggle for love, sex, and marriage" (33). He goes on to describe the actions of Marty, Grace, Suke, and Felice in some detail. Morrison also examines their respective relationships to and with Giles Winterborne and Edred Fitzpiers. The article is brief but logically organized, and Morrison's views are clearly presented.

The Turberville Window, Saint John the Baptist Church, Bere Regis, Dorset: "Over the tester of the bedstead was a beautifully traceried window of many lights, its date being the fifteenth century. It was called the d'Urberville Window, and in the upper part could be discerned heraldic emblems like those on Durbeyfield's old seal and spoon" (Chapter LII, *Tess of the d'Urbervilles*).

Chapter VII
Tess of the d'Urbervilles

Circumstances of Composition

Some of the principal ideas for the major elements of *Tess of the d'Urbervilles* came to Hardy during the time he lived with his wife Emma in the town of Sturminster Newton (Millgate 184-191). In describing Sturminster, Hardy biographer Michael Millgate says that "Sturminster, a market town of some 1,500 inhabitants, was the focal point for the eastern part of the Vale of Blackmoor, the 'Valley of the Little Dairies' of *Tess of the d'Urbervilles*" (185). Clearly then, Hardy borrowed the setting for a significant portion of the novel from Sturminster and the surrounding countryside.

In addition to the setting, other significant elements of the novel seem to have been generated by Hardy's experiences in Sturminster. While some critics refer to Hardy's cousin Tryphena Sparks, Hardy's grandmother Mary Head, or a dairywoman named Augusta Way as possible models for the character Tess, another woman who was involved in an incident which occurred during Hardy's stay in Sturminster seems to have led Hardy in his creation of Tess. Apparently, the Hardys (Thomas and Emma) had a servant named Jane (a Jenny Phillips is also mentioned) who left her situation with the Hardys as a result of an indiscretion involving a meeting with a young man. The Hardys learned some time later that Jane had become pregnant, and that her son had died shortly after birth. Interestingly, the child "had been privately baptized before its death—presumably by its mother" (191). This incident is strikingly similar to the scene recorded in the novel version of *Tess* when Tess chooses to baptize her baby Sorrow because the parson had refused her request for a Christian burial. Millgate says:

> Not only does Jenny Phillips's situation conform more closely to the narrative details of the novel than that of any other known "original," but Hardy's memories of her singing make her by far the likeliest possessor of the voice which is described as unforgettable by those who once heard it. (294)

In light of these observations, it is interesting to note that the incidents from the novel which appear to have been so closely linked to the life of an actual person were the cause of so much concern among Hardy's potential publishers.

Even before its initial publication in 1891, *Tess of the d'Urbervilles* was surrounded by controversy. When Hardy was still writing the first of several drafts, Tillotson Publishers, which had originally committed to publish the work, "took fright at the explicitness of the material and canceled their contract with Hardy" (Gibson 37). Hardy's attempts to find a new publisher proved unfruitful; thus, he was forced to delete or revise several passages before the novel was finally accepted for publication by the *Graphic* (37). Shortly after the serialized version appeared in "twenty-four weekly installments, from 4 July until 26 December 1891" (Laird 6), a three-volume edition of the novel was published with "most of the offending passages restored" (Casagrande xv). Subsequent editions reflect a variety of changes which Hardy made throughout his career and which were of interest to his contemporaries as well as the readers of today (Laird 4).

Due to the demands placed upon authors who provided materials considered unsuitable for serial publication, Hardy was forced to make a variety of concessions regarding certain elements of the novel *Tess* (Laird 5). There is a great deal of interest in the revisions made by Hardy, and one helpful source is the bibliography by Richard L. Purdy. Purdy's bibliography provides a comprehensive record of Hardy's publications, presenting the information in such a way as to render it especially useful to students of Hardy's major novels. He describes each volume in detail and includes notes filled with biographical, historical, and background information on the particular work being examined. The entries for *Tess of the d'Urbervilles* clearly outline the chronological development of the various publications and discuss the nature and scope of each text.

Another extremely helpful source is the work by John T. Laird. Laird's work, *The Shaping of "Tess of the d'Urbervilles,"* traces the line of transmission, examines the various chronological layers of the manuscript, and looks at the revisions made by Hardy in a very systematic and precise way. Specifically, Laird examines seven versions of the novel, of which three are most important: the manuscript as found in the British Museum, the serial version as printed in the *Graphic,* and the Wessex Edition published by Macmillan in 1912. Of primary interest to the readers of *Tess* are the five identifiable layers of the extant manuscript (20). The development of the text is particularly interesting because there seems to have been a conscious effort on Hardy's part to render the novel acceptable for serial publication in terms of form and content. Also, as Laird points out, Hardy was interested in improving the quality of the novel while keeping his ideas intact. This is significant because it may have led Hardy to develop subtle principles of inclusion and exclusion based on what might be deemed acceptable or unacceptable to his Victorian reading audience. Laird suggests that Hardy may have excluded information pertaining to incidents that may be perceived as immoral, but that he may have included information relating to incidents or scenes which might tend to create a sense of surprise or sensation (17).

Yet another interesting and helpful source is the work by Mary Ellen Chase. In *Thomas Hardy from Serial to Novel*, she looks at several aspects of the text and includes very specific information relating to alterations made in plot, setting, and characterization (Chase 71-105). In addition to examining major revisions in the text, Chase examines some of the minor changes such as alterations in sentence structure and grammar (107). Her approach is interesting because she identifies and describes in detail several passages from the serial version and compares them to related passages in the novel version. While Chase is unaware of some of the information regarding the definitive text as later outlined by Laird and Purdy, her study is useful because she looks at the changes that Hardy made in the novel to render it acceptable for publication in both the serial and the novel forms. While numerous sources refer to the alterations made by Hardy, Chase provides detailed information regarding the differences between the serial version of the text and the version which appeared in book form. She points out that two very significant portions of *Tess* were excluded from the version printed in the *Graphic*. However, the missing portions do appear as short stories under the titles of "Saturday Night in Arcady" printed in the *National Observer* and "The Midnight Baptism" printed in the *Fortnightly Review* (Rutland 224-226).

Since these two sections of the narrative are so powerful in themselves, and since they add a sense of coherence to the work, it is alarming to consider that they could have been excluded from the serial publication. Also, it is important to mention that to compensate for the missing incidents it was necessary for Hardy to alter specific conversations which took place between and among the various characters. In addition to making changes in certain dialogues, Hardy also changed the chronological arrangement of at least one significant event. These changes render the serial version of the novel far less satisfying in terms of plot and character development.

Works Cited

Casagrande, Peter J. *"Tess of the d'Urbervilles": Unorthodox Beauty*. New York: Twayne, 1992.

Chase, Mary Ellen. *Thomas Hardy from Serial to Novel*. New York: Russell and Russell, 1964.

Gibson, James. *"Tess of the d'Urbervilles." The Thomas Hardy Journal* 7.3 (1991): 34-47.

Laird, John T. *The Shaping of "Tess of the d'Urbervilles."* London: Oxford University Press, 1975.

Millgate, Michael. *Thomas Hardy: A Biography*. New York: Random House, 1982.

Purdy, Richard L. *Thomas Hardy: A Bibliographical Study*. Oxford: Clarendon Press, 1968.

Rutland, William R. *Thomas Hardy: A Study of His Writings and Their Background.* New York: Russell & Russell, 1962.

Atkins, N. F. *Hardy, Tess and Myself*. Beaminster: The Toucan Press, 1962.

This brief essay is a personal account written by the actor who played Alec d'Urberville in the 1924 stage production of Hardy's novel *Tess*. Atkins describes his initial feeling of excitement when asked to take the role of Alec and goes on to discuss his relationship with Thomas Hardy and his wife Florence. He also provides some background information regarding the various stage productions of *Tess* and insights about Thomas and Florence Hardy's reactions to these adaptations. This selection is of value because of its personal and reflective nature, but should be viewed as a somewhat subjective account of the events described.

Casagrande, Peter J. *"Tess of the d'Urbervilles": Unorthodox Beauty.* New York: Twayne, 1992.

The first section of this book provides a useful chronology of "Hardy's Life and Works." It also includes several useful chapters which outline the historical context in which the novel was written and which describe the circumstances of publication and critical reaction to Hardy's work. The second section (much larger than the first) is devoted to Casagrande's interpretation of the novel *Tess*. In discussing this work, Casagrande finds it necessary to create a new word which he feels best describes what he feels is "Hardy's insistence that the ugly is beautiful" (31). The term he creates is "beaugly" (28). This term presents a problem not only because it is an oxymoron but also because Casagrande seems unable to follow through with his arguments in support of the term. Rather than opening up the novel, the term "beaugly" casts a shadow over the interpretation of the novel which in turn colors the actions of the characters in an almost completely negative light. Each of the chapters which follow the section introducing the term "beaugly" addresses interesting ideas relating to the text, but Casagrande's repeated references to this term distort his primary argument.

Davis, William A. " 'But he can be prosecuted for this': Legal and Sociological Backgrounds of the Mock Marriage in Hardy's Serial *Tess." Colby Library Quarterly* 25.1 (1989): 28-41.

In his article, Davis deals with the version of *Tess* which was published in serial form. He explores one particular scene in detail and examines "Hardy's interest in legal matters" (28) as it relates to the "mock marriage" between Alec and Tess. Davis provides historical information regarding the legality of certain types of marriages, and he suggests that Hardy would have been aware of the legislation which was passed in an effort to prevent mock marriages from taking place. Davis points out that "the history of false marriage and the unlawful procurement of girls and women for carnal knowledge in eighteenth- and nineteenth-century England is both interesting (in legal works) and well documented" (32). He goes on to explain the reasoning behind Hardy's decision to add the mock marriage scene to the novel, asserting that it was carefully and thoughtfully done.

Ebbatson, Roger. "The Plutonic Master: Hardy and the Steam Threshing-Machine." *Critical Survey* 2.1(1990): 63-69.

Ebbatson's article focuses on his interpretation of the "Steam Threshing-Machine scene" in *Tess of the d'Urbervilles* (63). He begins by providing examples of the descriptive language used in the text of the novel and discussing interpretations of the scene which are at variance with his own in the sense that they focus on plot and character rather than on the "historical moment of the scene's genesis" (64). Ebbatson also provides historical information regarding the technological development of the steam threshing-machine and discusses the effects of this development upon the rural laborer. In order to support his materialist reading of the scene, Ebbatson cites the works of Karl Marx and comes to the conclusion that

> the impact of the tragic determinism which dominates Tess's career is, in the last analysis, to undermine that historic potential for collective endeavor which emerges with striking clarity in the records of the farm workers' lives in the nineteenth century. (67-68)

Overall, his arguments seem to be somewhat broader in scope than the limits of the particular scene in question would suggest. The assertions made by Ebbatson are insightful but could be more fully developed.

Fleissner, Robert F. "*Tess of the d'Urbervilles* and George Turberville." *Names* 37.1 (1989): 65-68.

Robert Fleissner is primarily interested in determining the source of the use of d'Urberville as Tess's last name. He begins by explaining how Hardy may have obtained information on George Turberville and how he may have become acquainted with his work. Fleissner suggests that just as George Turberville belongs to the Renaissance period, "*Tess* harks back to the Renaissance in several respects" as well. Fleissner points out that hunting and bird imagery appear throughout the novel, as does floral imagery. He also cites the work of Michael Millgate to substantiate his idea that the naming of characters was of great importance to Hardy, and that the linkage between the names Turberville and d'Urberville may be more than circumstantial.

Gibson, James. "*Tess of the d'Urbervilles.*" *The Thomas Hardy Journal* 7.3 (1991): 34-47.

A helpful introduction to the novel *Tess*, this article includes information about the original form of publication and the subsequent emendations to the text. Gibson provides information regarding the composition of the novel including alternative titles for it as well as original names chosen for the characters. Gibson goes on to explore the primary issues addressed in the novel and states that *Tess of the d'Urbervilles* is concerned with important questions of human behavior, and to read it is to "be brought into contact with a sensitive and comprehensive mind brooding over issues that are part of all our lives" (39). Some of the issues that Gibson discusses are love between a man and a woman, the importance of heredity, the role of fate, and the influence of social change. He also discusses Hardy's method of character development and its relationship to the structure of the novel. Gibson concludes his article by reiterating the strengths of the novel in terms of its organization, style, and content. The article serves as an excellent source of background information while it also provides some useful critical examination.

Kalikoff, Beth. "The Execution of Tess d'Urberville at Wintoncester." *Executions and the British Experience from the 17th to the 20th Century: A Collection of Essays*. Ed. William D. Thesing. Jefferson: McFarland, 1990. 111-121.

Kalikoff clearly states her intentions: she says that she wishes to "explore the cultural resonance of public execution in Thomas Hardy's late-Victorian classic, *Tess of the d'Urbervilles*" (111). Kalikoff describes "gallows street literature" (112) and provides evidence of its popularity. She also describes Hardy's interest in public hangings and discusses the details surrounding several of the hangings that he personally witnessed. She further discusses the way in which Hardy deals with his impressions of executions through the final scene in the novel *Tess*. This final scene is examined in some detail, and Kalikoff concludes her observations by stating that "the public execution of Tess d'Urberville lacerates and bonds the two gazers on the hill [Angel and Liza-Lu]. It completes an inexorable cycle of crime and punishment" (119). Her observations are interesting, as is the historical data which is provided. The article provides a unique interpretation regarding Hardy's interest in public executions in relationship to the novel *Tess*.

LaValley, Albert J., ed. *Twentieth-Century Interpretations of Tess of the d'Urbervilles*. Englewood Cliffs, NJ: Prentice Hall, 1969.

This volume includes numerous essays which address specific issues that arise within the novel *Tess of the d'Urbervilles*. In general, the individual selections are brief and present a viewpoint which is distinct from those expressed in the other essays. Some of the topics discussed by the various authors have to do with the nature of morality, humanity, heredity, and tragedy, as expressed through the novel *Tess*. One article of particular interest is the selection by Dorothy VanGhent. VanGhent closely examines the novel for evidence of Hardy's concern with the individual human experience in relationship to the collective experience of humanity. Also worth studying is the brief discussion by D. H. Lawrence in which he examines the nature of the characters Tess, Alec, and Angel. The book as a whole provides a useful collection of materials which present varying critical views.

Mallett, Phillip. " 'Smacked, and Brought to Her Senses': Hardy and the Clitheroe Abduction Case." *The Thomas Hardy Journal* 8.2 (1992): 70-73.

This article is devoted to the study of a particular court case which was taking place at the same time Hardy was completing the novel *Tess of the d'Urbervilles*. The case involved the abduction of a wife by her husband, and when it was brought to court the original ruling was in favor of the husband. Later, however, the ruling was overturned and the wife was permitted to return to her former residence apart from her husband. Mallet points out that the specific details of the case more closely resemble incidents related in the novel *Jude the Obscure* but also notes that the final scenes in *Tess* may in some way reflect Hardy's views regarding the rights of women as established through the final ruling in the Clitheroe Abduction Case.

Nunokawa, Jeff. "Tess, Tourism, and the Spectacle of the Woman." *Rewriting the Victorians: Theory, History and the Politics of Gender*. Ed. Linda M. Shires. New York: Routledge, 1992. 70-85.

Although Nunokawa's discussion of the novel *Tess* begins with a somewhat difficult and problematic focus involving the objectification of women as expressed through psychoanalytic theory, his assertions are soon understandable when the central issue relating to tourism is examined. Nunokawa argues that "Hardy's novel is a generic handbook for the tourist, gathering together in one volume the 'antique, ethnic and pristine' and scopes that form the object of his [Hardy's] attraction" (78). Nunokawa cites the works of Karl Baedeker, a tour book writer, as the source for some of Hardy's inspired descriptions of landscape. Apparently there is sufficient evidence to support this claim, and Nunokawa is able to provide several examples of descriptions from Baedeker's handbooks. The major premise of the article is interesting, as are Nunokawa's careful examinations of several key scenes from the novel. His assertion regarding the influence of tourism on Hardy's writing is intriguing and merits further critical discussion.

Stevens, Jack. "Literary and Biographical Allusion in *Tess of the d'Urbervilles.*" *The Thomas Hardy Yearbook* 14 (1987): 20-25.
   In an effort to show a link between the events in the novel *Tess* and Hardy's own life, Stevens provides specific background information about Hardy, his family, and his friends. He also points out that there are numerous allusions to *As You Like It* and *Oedipus Rex*. In reference to Hardy's friend, Horace Moule, and to Hardy's niece/cousin, Tryphena Sparks, Stevens relates both Alec's and Angel's reactions to Tess to Hardy's desertion of Tryphena, as well as Moule's apparent attraction to her. He goes so far as to say that "Hardy himself had put on a false cover of evangelicalism and morality, like Alec and Angel, to rationalize his own fear of society and the same 'moral hobgoblins' he tells Tess not to fear" (72). Stevens discusses the similarity between the role Alec plays in *Tess* and the role Duke Frederick plays in *As You Like It*. He cites other examples of similar elements in terms of character and plot, but he does point out that the end of the novel *Tess* is very different from the end of the play *As You Like It*. At this point, Stevens further discusses the structure of *Tess* as it relates to the five elements of Greek tragedy. He concludes by stating that "there is a very close relationship between Hardy's life and his art" (23). This argument seems to be brought out successfully by the background information provided as well as the numerous examples from the text of *Tess of the d'Urbervilles* itself.

Comparative Studies

Beach, Joseph Warren. *The Technique of Thomas Hardy*. New York: Russell and Russell, 1962.

Beach begins his discussion of *Tess of the d'Urbervilles* by summarizing the events of the plot. He claims that "The story of Tess is one of extreme simplicity" (180). He continues by comparing the plot organization in *Tess* to that of *The Return of the Native*, and he provides a condensed outline of Tess's story. Beach uses this comparison to point out the strengths in the novel *Tess of the d'Urbervilles*, which he feels is superior "not merely to *The Return of the Native*, but to any other English novel of its period" (185). He supports this assertion by taking the reader through the novel chronologically, while providing commentary on particular scenes which he feels are central to the novel's main theme. He concludes by reiterating what he feels Hardy was attempting to do in writing *Tess* and reminds readers of the pity that the story evokes.

Grimsditch, Herbert B. *Character and Environment in the Novels of Thomas Hardy*. New York: Russell and Russell, 1962.

This book essentially examines the *Wessex* novels. There are numerous references to *Tess* throughout the work which compare and contrast the various characters from each of the Wessex novels. These characters are also examined in view of the environment, which Grimsditch sees as a destined and powerful force in their development. He cites the general state of Tess's family as the chief reason for her failures: "the conditions of Tess's home life are the beginning of her sorrow and the culminating factor in bringing about her last and fatal surrender" (34). Later, Grimsditch reiterates this claim by discussing Tess's repeated refusals to accept help from Alec d'Urberville (152-154). Throughout the work he relies on certain portions of the novel *Tess* to support his overall assertions regarding this group of novels. The work provides a detailed discussion involving several novels and is useful because of its focus on Hardy's novels individually and as a group.

Holloway, John. *The Victorian Sage: Studies in Argument*. 1953. London: Macmillan, 1962.

Holloway begins his work by stressing the importance of thoroughly reading the introductory chapter of the book, since it provides a frame of reference for each subsequent chapter. In this introduction, Holloway identifies the aims of several major authors of the Victorian Period. He asserts that "interest of a general or speculative kind in what the world is like, where a man stands in it, and how he should live is perhaps the chief thing they have in common" (1). The authors to which Holloway is referring are Carlyle, Disraeli, Eliot, Newman, Arnold, and Hardy. In the chapter specifically devoted to Hardy's works, three subsections focus on Hardy's use of nature. In general, the chapter centers on what Holloway sees as the development of a sense of values which can be seen throughout Hardy's works. Holloway says, "it is true that the whole trend of one novel after another portrays this same scale of values. To adapt one's life to one's traditional situation is good, to uproot oneself for material ends is bad, to do so for romantic passion or an abstract ideal is if anything worse" (286). Holloway's study is interesting because it is comparative in nature; however, its scope is a bit broad to be contained in one book.

Howe, Irving. *Thomas Hardy*. London: Macmillan, 1967.

This book provides not only biographical information about Hardy but also some critical discussion of his works. The chapters titled "The World of Wessex" and "Let the Day Perish" are the most useful for students of *Tess*. When referring to the novel *Tess*, Howe says that "the book stands at the center of Hardy's achievement, if not as his greatest then certainly his most characteristic, and these readers or critics who cannot accept its emotional ripeness must admit that for them Hardy is not a significant novelist" (110). He goes on to discuss the attributes which make Tess, as an individual and as a character, memorable as well as enduring. His discussion of the novel is thorough and useful because it is holistic in its approach, yet detailed enough to establish a sense of coherence in terms of its arguments.

Humm, Maggie. "Gender and Narrative in Thomas Hardy." *The Thomas Hardy Yearbook* 11 (1984): 41-48.

Humm compares the character of Tess from *Tess of the d'Urbervilles* with Sue Bridehead from *Jude the Obscure*. She works largely from the premise that "neither Tess nor Sue has the traditional identity of women in fiction" (42). She also explores the nature of Victorian attitudes regarding the role of women in society. Further, she examines the ways in which these attitudes affect Hardy's own hypotheses, asserting that in creating characters like Tess and Sue, "Hardy was hypothesizing an alternative image of social attitude" (43). However, Humm goes on to point out that while Hardy's writings raise many questions about the validity of a number of Victorian social attitudes, he does not provide any answers. Nevertheless, Humm comes to the conclusion that perhaps asking the questions was sufficient.

Jagdish, Chandra Dave. *The Human Predicament in Hardy's Novels.* London: Macmillan, 1985.

Jagdish conducts a somewhat complicated and difficult discussion regarding "Hardy's vision of the world as manifested in a series of his novels" (3). Initially, he examines Hardy's unique philosophical outlook as well as his metaphysical and mystical perspectives. In his exploration of *Tess*, Jagdish further inspects Hardy's ideas as they are reflected in his writing. After vividly describing Tess's predicament regarding the baby Sorrow, he says that "customary morality is not, according to Hardy, the right and reasoned ethical response of the collective mass of the pitiable cries of the 'units' of society in distress" (153). Jagdish goes on to discuss ethical responses customarily postulated in religion through Angel as well as his father, "Old Mr. Clare" (154-155). He concludes his arguments on the novel by summarizing the essence of Hardy's view as expressed through his characters. Overall, his treatment of the novel is interesting, if somewhat complicated and jargon-filled.

Meisel, Perry. *Thomas Hardy: The Return of the Repressed.* New Haven, CT: Yale University Press, 1972.

In his examination of the major fictional works by Thomas Hardy, Meisel states that "the primary characteristic of his fiction is its tension—a tension that permeates the development of his universe in prose and that lends a distinctly historical aspect to his work" (1). Throughout his discussion of *Tess* (chapter 6), he develops this argument by citing specific examples from the novel. He identifies the source of tension in the novel as Tess's alienation from society (119). Meisel further points to scenes such as Tess's arrival at Talbothays Dairy and her initial meeting of Alec d'Urberville. There are also references to Tess's attempts "to mediate between the extremes of Angel and Alec, each of whom represents an individualized alienation from the community—one through a surfeit of intellectualism, the other through material overabundance" (129). Meisel is able to support his assertions thoroughly and consistently through an abundance of examples from the novel. He provides a clear, concise discussion of *Tess of the d'Urbervilles*.

Miller, J. Hillis. *Thomas Hardy: Distance and Desire*. Cambridge, MA: Harvard University Press, 1970.

There are many references to *Tess of the d'Urbervilles* throughout Miller's book. The purpose of the book as a whole is to examine the themes of "distance and desire." Miller argues that

> Two themes are woven throughout the totality of Hardy's work and may be followed from one edge of it to the other as outlining threads: distance and desire—distance as the source of desire and desire as the energy behind attempts to turn distance into closeness. (xii)

Miller discusses *Tess* in relation to other works by Hardy and re-emphasizes the importance of the overriding themes of "distance and desire." He comments upon the ways in which the forces of nature intensify desire as well as the way in which history creates distance between Tess and her ability to choose her own actions. Other topics addressed include the influence of time, fate, and justice. In general, Miller is clear in his presentation, but the scope of his arguments is very broad and therefore it is difficult to connect some of the references to specific works.

Pinion, F. B. *A Hardy Companion: A Guide to the Works of Thomas Hardy and Their Background*. London: Macmillan, 1968.

Pinion's work includes a variety of information which is useful to the student of Hardy's works. Included in the work are an extensive chronology of Hardy's life; a section devoted to a discussion of each of Hardy's novels, short stories, and poems; and several sections or chapters which explore Hardy's views on topics such as art, tragedy, Christianity, and politics. Also set forth in the text is a "Dictionary of People and Places in Hardy's Works" (225). The references to specific novels which occur throughout the text deal primarily with their relationship to other works by Hardy or with the circumstances of composition. The photographs and maps contained in the "companion" serve as points of reference for the reader who is not familiar with Hardy's background or with his creation of *Wessex*. The specific references to *Tess of the d'Urbervilles* provide insights regarding Hardy's possible intention in writing the novel as well as its relationship to his other works.

Springer, Marlene. *Hardy's Use of Allusion*. Lawrence: University Press of Kansas, 1983.

Springer discusses many of Thomas Hardy's works. She begins with a discussion of Hardy's style in general and then focuses on specific works in subsequent chapters. The final chapter addresses Hardy's use of allusion in the novels *Tess* and *Jude the Obscure*. Included in the chapter is a brief history of the various editions of *Tess* as well as specific references to the subtitle "A Pure Woman." After this brief introduction, Springer outlines the types of allusion used by Hardy and gives several examples of each type. Her examination of the text is thorough and offers many insights regarding the significance of certain passages within the novel. She closes her arguments by re-emphasizing the importance of recognizing the various allusions used by Hardy. She says that

> Hardy drew from many worlds to enlarge his own novelistic universe, making his allusions serve his audience as avenues into his fiction. He requires of his readers that they bring to his novels an imaginative effort, that they read as connoisseurs. (174)

Stout, Janis P. "The Fallen Woman and the Conflicted Author: Hawthorne and Hardy." *American Transcendental Quarterly* 1.3 (1987): 233-246.
The article investigates the differences between Thomas Hardy's and Nathaniel Hawthorne's attempts to challenge stereotypes regarding women and chastity or purity. Stout argues that while Hawthorne does create female characters like Hester Prynne and Zenobia who challenge the Victorian notion that a woman is either completely good or completely evil based on her sexual experiences, Hardy more effectively challenges this notion through the character Tess. Stout carefully considers the ways in which Hardy develops Tess as a character and the ways in which the omniscient narrator provides information that gives the reader a more complete knowledge of Tess's intentions as well as her actions. Stout concludes the article by offering three interpretations of the subtitle given by Hardy, which asserts that Tess is a pure woman. The three possibilities suggested by Stout are:

1. Initially Tess is pure, but she is cheated of this purity by others.
2. Tess remains pure even after her sexual experience because her intentions were pure.
3. The subtitle asserts the essential purity of nature and therefore of sexuality, which is part of nature. (245-246)

Each of the interpretations invites further evaluation, and even Stout is reluctant to choose one above the others.

Swann, Charles. "A Hardy Debt to Hawthorne." *Notes and Queries* 6 (1992): 188-189.

In this brief selection, Swann considers two incidents which occur in *Tess*, and which are strikingly similar to two incidents recounted in the novel *The Scarlet Letter* by Nathaniel Hawthorne. Swann compares a scene involving Angel Clare and Mercy Chant to a scene from Hawthorne's novel which includes Reverend Dimmesdale and an anonymous woman from his congregation. He also discusses the similarities in the conversation between Angel and Tess and the dialogue between Reverend Dimmesdale and Hester on life after death. Swann simply asserts that while the scenes are not identical, they are at least similar enough to warrant close inspection or examination.

Nature of the Novel

Beckingham, Cushla R. "The Importance of Family in Hardy's Fictional World." *The Thomas Hardy Journal* 5.2 (1985): 62-68.

Beckingham's article provides a brief discussion of Hardy's views regarding the importance of heredity as it is addressed in his poetry and in his novels. A variety of Victorian ideologies are discussed and examples of the ways in which these ideologies are reflected in Hardy's works are provided. Beckingham focuses on "familism" as an environmental force which exerts pressure on the individual but does point out that Hardy's view of heredity was, like his view of other forces, a response to what he read and believed, rather than consistent exposition or elucidation of the science of heredity itself (64). Also included in the article are several specific examples of Hardy's views as they relate to the text of *Tess of the d'Urbervilles*. Overall, the article is successful in its attempt to address issues relating to the significance of family in Hardy's works.

Blank, Paula C. "*Tess of the d'Urbervilles*: The English Novel and the Foreign Plot." *Mid-Hudson Language Studies* 12 (1989): 62-71.

This article examines the novel primarily in terms of its form. Blank refers to Hardy's views on novel writing and attempts to explain the ways in which his views manifest themselves within the framework of *Tess of the d'Urbervilles*. Blank also points out that the novel is filled with various allusions to literature of the past, but she does not seem to consider this as one of the novel's strengths. She goes on to state that along with the use of allusion, Hardy has mingled themes which are reminiscent of the romance novel. Blank goes so far as to say that "Hardy's novel at once parodies the inherited conventions of romance and stands as a testimony to their enduring influence" (67). To support her ideas, she cites examples from the text while providing further evidence of Hardy's own thoughts regarding the nature of the novel in general. The article concludes by asserting that perhaps Hardy was less than effective in his attempt to create a new novel in a new form. The article is interesting, and its premise is plausible.

Ellis, Reuben. "Joan Durbeyfield Writes to Margaret Saville: An Intermediary Reader in Thomas Hardy's *Tess of the d'Urbervilles*." *Colby Library Quarterly* 24.1 (1988): 14-26.

Ellis presents an alternative view of *Tess* in that he suggests the possibility of reading *Tess* as an epistolary novel. He closely examines the letters which actually appear in the text and the letters which are only mentioned by the various characters. Ellis refers to the novels *Clarissa*, *Humphry Clinker*, *Werther*, and *Frankenstein*. He says that "just as the letter addresses near the beginning of Mary Shelley's *Frankenstein* demand that we acknowledge an intermediary presence in that novel, the epigraph to *Tess* invites us to invent a similar presence/absence as a fictional audience to the novel's letter" (22). Ellis also refers to the different drafts of *Tess* and concludes by examining the influence of the narrator in shaping the novel. His suggestions regarding the possible epistolary format of *Tess* are interesting and thought provoking.

Higonnet, Margaret R. "Fictions of Feminine Voice: Antiphony and Silence in Hardy's *Tess of the d'Urbervilles*." *Out of Bounds: Male Writers and Gender(ed) Criticism*. Ed. Laura Claridge. Amherst: University of Massachusetts Press, 1990. 197-218.

In her article, Higonnet deals primarily with Hardy's use of the narrator and the ways in which this narrator gives "voice" to Tess's story (198). She argues that from the outset, "Hardy maps a repressive set of discourses that are inadequate to true morality and inimical to the development and expression of Tess's true selfhood" (200). She continues her discussion by pointing out how Alec and Angel fail to understand Tess's words as well as her actions. In addition, Higonnet describes Tess's development as a character as expressed through her voice as well as the voice of the narrator. She concludes by examining the significance of silence in relationship to the narrator's ability to tell Tess's story because Tess cannot. Higonnet's article is effective in its attempt to explore the issue of the feminine voice in the novel. It is thorough and well thought out; however, some of the terms are technical, and a second reading may be necessary.

Hornback, Bert G. *The Metaphor of Chance.* Athens: Ohio University Press, 1971.

Hornback establishes his purpose early. He says that his "plan is to examine Hardy's setting, in space and in time, as it exists in itself, as it supports the major characters, and as it is used to establish the literal (physical) and metaphorical environment for his themes" (4). He begins by examining some of Hardy's poetry and then the minor novels. Somewhat later, he looks at three of the major works: *The Mayor of Casterbridge*, *Jude the Obscure*, and *Tess of the d'Urbervilles*. In his treatment of *Tess*, Hornback states that "Tess's tragic fault is her seduction by Alec d'Urberville" (111). This argument can only be supported by a narrow reading of the early events of the novel and a limited analysis of Tess as a character. Several interesting points are discussed; nevertheless, it is difficult to accept Hornback's arguments as definitive because he fails to point out specific passages that indicate that Tess may have been raped rather than simply seduced.

Hyman, Virginia R. *Ethical Perspective in the Novels of Thomas Hardy.* New York: Kennikat Press, 1975.

This book is devoted to a thorough study of Hardy's ideas about writing as well as the writings themselves. The first several chapters address Hardy's evolution as a thinking man and also discuss the development of his ideas as they relate to the creation of the characters in his fiction. The chapter titled "Character as Ethical Type" is of particular interest. This chapter provides a great deal of information about Victorian ideas and helps the reader become more aware of the prevailing philosophies of the time. Later chapters discuss individual characters and frequently refer to the information presented in chapter 3. The two chapters devoted to Tess work from the premise that Tess is naturally passive. Hyman goes so far as to say that "it is this natural passivity, inherited from her parents, that is to be Tess's downfall" (108). She continues by discussing how Tess's natural passivity makes her more and more vulnerable to Alec and then to Angel. In addition to the chapters specifically devoted to *Tess,* Hyman includes a chapter which discusses the development of Angel as a character. In her discussion of Angel, Hyman continues to refer to Tess and the effect she has had upon Clare. Her arguments are well thought out and are consistent throughout the individual sections.

Kramer, Dale. *Thomas Hardy, the Forms of Tragedy.* Detroit: Wayne State University Press, 1975.

Kramer examines a number of novels written by Thomas Hardy. He specifically looks at the various ways in which the elements of tragedy appear throughout these works. He devotes an entire chapter to his discussion of *Tess,* in which he argues that *"Tess of the d'Urbervilles* stresses the subjectivity of experience and judgment" (112). He further states that

> Hardy establishes subjectivity as the basis of perceiving the novel's action through a variety of methods, whose effect is to turn the individual upon himself for judgments and to deny the usefulness and trustworthiness of external perceptions and moralities. (115)

To support his claims, Kramer gives many lengthy examples from the text of the novel, followed by explanation. He refers to Tess's and Angel's actions as they occur in response to a given circumstance and concludes by restating his assertion that *Tess of the d'Urbervilles* can be read as a tragedy.

Sommers, Jeffrey. "Hardy's Other Bildungsroman: *Tess of the d'Urbervilles." English Literature in Transition, 1880-1920* 25 (1982): 159-168.

Sommers is careful to define the term *bildungsroman* at the outset of his article. He also includes definitions of other terms which have been used to describe the nature of the novel *Tess.* He asserts that *Tess* should be read as a *bildungsroman* because it contains the elements implied by the term. Sommers outlines each of the criteria that serves to define the nature of a *bildungsroman*, and he goes on to describe the various motifs which Hardy uses to achieve his aim of creating a novel of growth. The three motifs discussed by Sommers are confinement, movement or flight, and dreams (161-163). Included with his discussion of each motif are numerous examples from the text. The examples are generally examined chronologically and serve to illustrate the unity of the novel. Sommers states his position openly and supports his arguments logically as well as effectively.

Wickens, G. Glenn. "Sermons in Stones: The Return to Nature in *Tess of the d'Urbervilles.*" *English Studies in Canada* 14.2 (1988): 184-203.

Wickens suggests that critics have found "confusion rather than complexity" when examining *Tess of the d'Urbervilles*. He argues against interpretations of the novel that would demand that the narrator's view should remain consistent throughout the work, and he further points out that it is precisely the varying positions taken by the narrator that give the novel its dialogic nature. In addition, he states that the "allusion is a literary mode for Hardy and *Tess* [is] an allusion novel." Wickens refers specifically to Shakespeare's *As You Like It* and to Wordsworth's *Prelude* while pointing out that as in these two works, there is evidence of a complex pastoral structure. Overall, the article is very effective. Wickens's approach to the novel is clearly stated, and his assertions are supported by numerous examples from the text. Nevertheless, his arguments do become increasingly complicated as the article progresses and therefore a close reading is essential.

Salient Features of the Novel

Claridge, Laura. "Tess: A Less than Pure Woman Ambivalently Presented." *Texas Studies in Literature and Language: A Journal of the Humanities* 28 (1986): 324-337.

Claridge deals primarily with what she perceives to be the greatest flaw in Hardy's *Tess of the d'Urbervilles*. She states that

> Hardy's intense identification with his heroine creates an almost compulsive authorial exoneration of Tess's mistakes, mistakes that instead must function as signs of the heroine's moral culpability if the novel's unity is to be maintained. (324)

After clearly stating her initial arguments, Claridge cites specific examples from the text which seem to support the notion that there is an inherent weakness in the approach taken by Hardy's narrator. She feels that the novel fails to establish and maintain a sense of coherence. As a result, she views the novel as a failure. Although she makes some interesting points in her examination of the text, her observations appear to be somewhat narrow and shortsighted. In addition, Claridge does not seem to take into account the audience for whom *Tess* was written, nor does she consider the various forms of its publication. Overall, her treatment of the novel appears to skim the surface of careful investigation.

Higonnet, Margaret R., ed. *The Sense of Sex: Feminist Perspectives on Hardy.* Chicago: University of Illinois Press, 1993.

This collection of essays is important not only because it is recent but also because it brings together a number of articles written with a feminist point of view in mind. Two of the selections are specifically devoted to discussing *Tess of the d'Urbervilles,* and one article, titled "Textual Hysteria: Hardy's Narrator on Women" by Kristin Brady, is devoted to examining the similarities of the "narratorial position" in many of the novels (87). Dianne Sadoff focuses on the development of the narrative form. Sadoff is referring to the character Tess when she says that "Hardy's heroine undertakes a narrative trajectory that appropriates, complicates and reverses the seduction plot to demonstrate its duplicity for the female subject" (149). In addition, she examines Roman Polanski's film interpretation of Hardy's novel. The selections contained in this collection are lengthy and somewhat complicated. Nevertheless, they are, in general, clearly written and address issues which generate discussion and help the reader better understand the narrator's role in *Tess of the d'Urbervilles.*

Lothe, Jakob. "Hardy's Authorial Narrative Method in *Tess of the d'Urbervilles.*" *The Nineteenth-Century British Novel.* Ed. Jeremy Hawthorne. Baltimore: Edward Arnold, 1986. 157-170.

As the title suggests, Lothe centers on the function of the narrator in *Tess of the d'Urbervilles.* He begins by discussing the previous criticism and points out that "although it is now a commonplace narrative theory that it is essential not to confuse author and narrator, some critics of Hardy continue to do so" (159). To strengthen his position, Lothe cites the works of critics who deal with the narrator of *Tess* as distinct from Hardy as author. He continues by identifying and describing the methods used by the narrator throughout the novel. In doing so, Lothe provides many examples from the text and offers explanation following each example. The terminology used by Lothe is somewhat technical, but a thorough reading of the article will shed much light on the significance of the methods used by the narrator of *Tess*.

Morrison, Ronald D. "Reading and Restoration in *Tess of the d'Urbervilles.*" *Victorian Newsletter* 82 (1992): 27-35.

This article approaches the novel in terms of past criticisms, and it deals primarily with the function of the narrator as an advocate of Tess's purity. Morrison begins by examining the parallels which seem to exist between *Tess* and Shakespeare's *Two Gentlemen of Verona*. The remaining portion of the article focuses on the attempts which Hardy, the narrator, and Angel Clare make to restore Tess's wounded name. Morrison links Hardy's views to those of his narrator, and he also contends that certain parts of the narration are incomplete. Therefore, the reader is forced to complete them using his or her own imagination (29). Morrison goes on to say that Hardy's narrator "also attempts to direct his reader through a series of emotions." In addition, he argues that when the novel comes to a close, Hardy's narrator has attempted to absolve Tess from her responsibility regarding her own actions. In other words, to establish Tess's purity and restore her wounded name, Morrison asserts that Hardy even brings Angel Clare's views in line with his own. Since Hardy, the narrator, and Angel can now accept Tess as being a mere victim of circumstances, this would seem to lead the reader to the same conclusion. However, Morrison encourages the reader to interpret Tess's character for himself or herself while at the same time considering Hardy's intentions as important.

Parker, Lynn. " 'Pure Woman' and Tragic Heroine? Conflicting Myths in Hardy's *Tess of the d'Urbervilles.*" *Studies in the Novel* 24.3 (1992): 273-280.

Parker addresses Hardy's possible reliance on folk ballads as a framework for the plot of *Tess of the d'Urbervilles*. She suggests that "if Hardy did indeed frame *Tess* loosely around the ballads . . . the inevitability of Tess's story becomes located within the constraints of an earlier tradition" (279). Parker also examines the significance of the subtitle added by Hardy, which asserts that Tess is "a pure woman." She states that Hardy's overt narrative impulse to declare Tess's innocence is immediately undercut by his narrative descriptions which mark her as "fallen" (277). Parker concludes by reiterating her claim that presenting Tess as a tragic heroine as well as a "pure woman" confuses the theme of the novel. The numerous examples she cites add to the ongoing discussion of the novel.

Pettit, Charles P. C. "Hardy's Concept of Purity in *Tess of the d'Urbervilles.*" *The Thomas Hardy Journal* 7.3 (1991): 48-57.

Pettit explores the significance of the subtitle "A Pure Woman," added by Hardy after his examination of the final proofs. He provides a current definition of purity and contrasts it with the Victorian concept as well as with Hardy's own interpretation of the term. Pettit argues that Hardy "is claiming as pure a heroine who is seduced/raped, has an illegitimate baby, marries without telling her husband of her past, returns to her first lover, and finally kills him" (50). This paradox, Pettit claims, accounts not only for the mixed reviews of the work by contemporary critics but also for the mixed response from the public. Pettit further notes that Hardy was surprised by the concern over his novel but maintained the subtitle as the primary indicator of the focus of the novel. Pettit supports his view with examples from the text as well as background information regarding Hardy's own concept of purity.

Silverman, Kaja. "History, Figuration, and Female Subjectivity in *Tess of the d'Urbervilles.*" *Novel* 18.1 (1984): 4-28.

The focus of Silverman's article is the narrator's delineation of Tess as a female character. The purpose of the article is rather unclear, but it seems that Silverman is arguing that Hardy's narrator vacillates between his representation of Tess as a figure in her own right and as a figurative representation of her as seen through the eyes of Angel and Alec. She also discusses the nature of Hardy's use of descriptive language and comments that "All the great utopian moments of the novel consist of tableaux in which spatial relations are so blurred and confused as to be unreadable, or where horizontal movements take priority over vertical ones" (15-16). Silverman's approach to the novel is unnecessarily complicated with separate arguments which do not seem to relate to her final conclusions. There are numerous interesting points made, but the overall premise is not apparent until the end of the article.

Character Analysis

Adamson, Jane. "Tess, Time, and Its Shapings." *The Critical Review* 26 (1984): 18-36.

Adamson begins her discussion by citing the works of several critics to point out certain consistencies in current criticism and to lead into her own interpretation of the novel's central focus. She says that

> Few English novels evoke a stronger sense of time's unstoppable momentum, of the natural progression of centuries, years, seasons, days, and hours. And this sense of time's impersonal pressure merges with the novel's creation of people personally experiencing it. (18)

In looking at the important influence of time, Adamson also examines the ways in which the characters in the novel perceive themselves, their actions, and the actions of characters other than themselves. Tess and Angel and their relationship dominate her discussion. Adamson points out that their relationship could have evolved differently if they had been able to perceive the possibility of shaping time through specific action. Nevertheless, Tess and Angel "construe their experience in one way or the other, either in terms of absolute determinism or in terms of a kind of absolute moral freedom and responsibility" (33). As a result, they separate in life and in death. The arguments presented in this article are thoroughly discussed and clearly presented. Adamson is successful in her attempt to identify time as a central theme in the novel, and she provides many examples from the text which support her initial premise.

Campbell, Elizabeth. "*Tess of the d'Urbervilles*: Misfortune Is a Woman." *The Victorian Newsletter* 76 (1989): 1-5.

Campbell begins her arguments by analyzing chapter 10 in *Tess of the d'Urbervilles*, discussing the nature of the scene involving Tess's journey to Chaseborough and her lack of participation in the dance which takes place that evening. Campbell says that this scene is important because

> Not only does it resonate with meaning for the entire novel by demonstrating Hardy's typical method of escalating the tragedy; it also shows how his tragic portrayal of timing has special significance for

twentieth-century readers concerned with gender relationships and human sexuality. (1)

She further supports her claims by relating this scene to various events which occur throughout the novel. She examines the text from part to whole and concludes by offering insights regarding the significant influence of Victorian ideologies on Hardy's development of Tess as a character. The article is straightforward in its presentation, and it provides many interesting observations with respect to the nature of Tess's dilemma as a character who is caught between the world of the past and the world of the future.

Freeman, Janet. "Ways of Looking at *Tess.*" *Studies in Philology* 79.3 (1982): 311-323.

This article presents a general overview which stresses the importance of Tess as an enduring fictional character. Freeman asserts that "watching Tess is the most fundamental and uncompromising demand Hardy makes on those who read about her" (311). She goes on to describe the ways in which various characters in the novel attempt to define Tess in their own terms, claiming that "none of them sees her as she is" (315). This failure to see Tess clearly is the basis for many of the conflicts which continue to surface throughout the novel. The relationship between Tess's views and Hardy's is also explored, and the reader is asked to consider Hardy's views as essential because they account for the attentiveness in the narrator's view of Tess.

Gatrell, Simon. "Angel Clare's Story." *The Thomas Hardy Journal* 7.3 (1991): 58-83.

This is an interesting account of the story from Angel Clare's perspective. Gatrell writes using Angel's first-person voice to lend a certain realistic quality to the piece. The narrator, presumably the living prototype for Angel Clare, begins by describing himself at the time of his arrival at Talbothays. The narrator reports his early perceptions of Tess and follows their relationship sequentially through the novel. As he does this he also points out what he feels to be the shortcomings in Hardy's representation of his character. These interjections add a touch of subtle humor while also demonstrating Gatrell's thorough knowledge of the various drafts of the novel. Gatrell concludes the article with the following statements supposedly made by Clare:

At the last all I can feel is that if I had been wiser; if my love had been as self-consuming as Tess's; if even I could have kept always in my mind my father's charity; then Tess and I would be flourishing still, together. (83)

Gatrell provides a unique account of the events described in the novel, and he clearly invites readers to consider new possibilities in their reading of *Tess*.

Greenslade, William. "The Lure of Pedigree in *Tess of the d'Urbervilles*." *The Thomas Hardy Journal* 7.3 (1991): 103-115.

Greenslade deals primarily with Hardy's interest in heredity. He states that "the sense of connection with the past was experienced as Hardy felt it to be—a kind of intolerable loss, which might be resolved through a very late-Victorian kind of appropriation, a tracing back of origins" (103). He relates this concern to specific areas in *Tess*, arguing that "the myth of pedigree to which the Durbeyfields blindly adhere, in the hope that it will be their deliverance, hastens their disintegration" (105). Greenslade differentiates between Tess's and Angel's interpretations of the importance of heritage and concludes by explaining the effects these views have on Tess specifically. Greenslade's observations are clearly identified, and the information presented provides a more comprehensive understanding of the novel and character *Tess*.

Morgan, Rosemarie. "Passive Victim? *Tess of the d'Urbervilles*." *The Thomas Hardy Journal* 5.1 (1989): 31-54.

Morgan begins the article by describing the ways in which the character Tess is misrepresented by critics who claim that Tess is overly passive or lacking in sexuality. Morgan challenges the notion that Tess merely succumbs to circumstances or fate: "Far from being a passive victim, Tess embodies a fierce impulse of self-determination against daunting, and ultimately insurmountable, odds" (35). She also distinguishes between the terms *repression* and *submission* as they relate to the assertions that Tess is innately passive. In addition, Morgan points out that Angel's moral weakness is far greater than Tess's. She further adds that "Angel, to a far greater extent than Tess, is formed and shaped by his past" (51). Morgan provides numerous examples from the text to support her arguments and is successful in her presentation of Tess as a complicated and complete character.

Pettit, Charles P. C. "Hardy's Vision of the Individual in *Tess of the d'Urbervilles*." *New Perspectives on Thomas Hardy*. Ed. Charles P. C. Pettit. New York: St. Martin's Press, 1994. 172-190.

In this selection, Pettit focuses on Tess and the way in which Hardy's use of varying narrative points of view help to reveal her character. Pettit also discusses how the shifts in narrative perspective help readers come to know Tess as an individual and as a member of society. He goes on to describe how the narrative viewpoint changes throughout the novel, and says that "frequently the viewpoint zooms in and out with no mention of an observer" (188). Therefore, Tess is often seen from two perspectives: that of the first- and third-person narrator. Pettit says:

> In *Tess* Hardy succeeds in using the very tension and interplay between the two perspectives to create his own vision, enriching the novel's perceptions further through the use of a wide variety of complementary visual angles. (188)

There are many references to the text of the novel, and Pettit provides numerous examples that serve to support his claims.

Ponsford, Michael. "Thomas Hardy's Control of Sympathy in *Tess of the d'Urbervilles*." *The Midwest Quarterly* 27.4 (1986): 487-503.

Ponsford addresses two central issues which he feels are generally agreed on in current critical discussion: "The first is that the book has a greater emotional appeal than any of Hardy's other works. . . . The second observation is that more than any of the other novels, *Tess* is dominated by a single character" (487). He notes that readers remain sympathetic to Tess throughout the novel, and that this sympathy is controlled by the narrator. Ponsford also identifies and examines several of the major themes in the novel as they are unified in Tess. The importance of the various settings is also addressed in terms of their relationship to the chronologically developed events which occur in the novel. Through his discussion of the major elements, Ponsford is able to support successfully his initial claims regarding the "emotional appeal" of the novel as well as the assertion that Tess is certainly the dominating character.

Veidemanis, Gladys V. "*Tess of the d'Urbervilles*: What the Film Left Out." *The English Journal* 77.7 (1988): 53-57.

This article reviews Roman Polanski's film version of *Tess*. Veidemanis admits that "the film is visually stunning" and points out that the "minor characters are wonderfully alive and visually engaging" (53). Nevertheless, she argues that the overall effect produced by the film falls short of the impressions generated by the reading of the novel itself. Veidemanis says that in Polanski's version "There is no sense of desperation, of being driven to the limits of human endurance" (55), whereas in the novel, Tess comes across as being in extremely desperate circumstances. Yet, even in view of the film's weakness, Veidemanis suggests that students may want to view the film for the purpose of conducting a comparative analysis.

St. Mary's Church, Fawley, Berkshire: "a tall new building of modern Gothic design, unfamiliar to English eyes, had been erected on a new piece of ground" (Chapter I.-i., *Jude the Obscure*).

Chapter VIII
Jude the Obscure

Circumstances of Composition

Like most of Hardy's novels, *Jude the Obscure* has an interesting composition and publication history. Aside from having used or suggested at least four different titles for the novel (*The Simpletons*, *Hearts Insurgent*, *The Recalcitrants*, and *Jude the Obscure*), Hardy also altered other aspects of the novel throughout the various stages of its development (, 29). A much bowdlerized version was printed in serial form beginning in December of 1894, and a somewhat restored version appeared in book form late in 1895 with a postdating of 1896. Yet, even though Hardy had been concerned about the direction his work had taken during the writing process, he, as Michael Millgate points out, was not aware that this particular work would generate such a strong response from his reviewers. Millgate succinctly states:

> Hardy was indeed unprepared for the depth, extent and directness of the hostility which marked many of the reviews of his novel. 368

Current critics refer to Hardy's own comments regarding the responses of his readers and reviewers as being directly responsible for Hardy's abandonment of novel writing in favor of poetry. Margaret Mahar observes that "With his final novel, *Jude the Obscure*, Thomas Hardy made his escape from narrative form" (303).

This last novel, along with the others, has inspired readers to search for Hardy's sources of inspiration. The link between Christminster and Oxford has been widely noted, and the original for Marygreen has been recognized as Fawley, the home of Hardy's paternal grandmother (Southerington 64). The settings described in the novel are unique because they extend the borders of *Wessex* as a fictional territory. In addition to identifying specific real-life locations for the towns and cities that appear in the novel, much speculation has occurred regarding the originals for the major characters. Sue is commonly thought to have been modeled after several women. In his somewhat dated article, F. R. Southerington expresses his doubt that there is a "need to look further than Tryphena for the model of Sue Bridehead" (67), Tryphena being, as noted in previous sections, one of Hardy's favorite nieces/cousins. However, Hardy biographer Michael Millgate notes that in actuality there seem to be very few similarities between the events that occur in Tryphena's life and the events that transpire in Sue's. Rather, Millgate would suggest that Sue is most likely a composite of traits associated with Florence Henniker (Hardy's friend), Mary Hardy (Hardy's sister), Tryphena Sparks, as well as others (350-353). Millgate points out that by Hardy's insistence upon using as "Sue's full name Susanna Florence Mary Bridehead, Hardy was thus incorporating an acknowledgment of his principal 'sources' for her characterization" (353).

As opposed to the varying views regarding Hardy's sources of inspiration for Sue's character, most seem to agree that the creation of Jude can be linked to Hardy's close associations with Horace Moule and John Antell (Millgate 346). Horace Moule's suicide and John Antell's frustrated attempts to gain an education seem to be reflected not only in the formation of Jude's character but also in the formation of Jude's story. In her article titled "A Short Story Prelude to *Jude the Obscure*: More Light on the Genesis of Hardy's Last Novel," Patricia Alden refers to Hardy's personal notes as well as to his "Preface to the First Edition" of *Jude* where Hardy indicates that he had for a long time been thinking about writing a story about a young man who wanted to obtain an education but would ultimately fail to achieve his goal (45-46). She states that Hardy's own remark "suggests that the theme of frustrated academic ambitions provided the original spark of inspiration for the novel" (46). She goes on to describe a very interesting link between the ideas presented in the novel *Jude the Obscure* and the ideas that surface in a short story published by Hardy some years prior. In referring to the short story, titled "A Tragedy of Two Ambitions," and to *Jude the Obscure*, Alden states, "Both the story and the novel take seriously the situation of the intelligent, industrious, scholarly poor man barred from the prestigious university he aspires to enter" (48). To further support her observations, she goes on to describe the basic plot structure of each of the two works while she also describes various similarities between Jude and the two young men featured in the short story. For a more complete study of the development of the manuscript, the article titled "The Evolution of *Jude the Obscure*" by Patricia Ingham is recommended. In her article, Ingham describes the development of Jude's story in great detail. She traces changes made in the manuscript throughout the composition process and discusses the differences between the serial version and the book version of the novel.

Works Cited

Alden, Patricia. "A Short Story Prelude to *Jude the Obscure*: More Light on the Genesis of Hardy's Last Novel." *The Colby Library Quarterly* 19.1 (1983): 45-52.

Ingham, Patricia. "The Evolution of *Jude the Obscure*." *The Review of English Studies* 27 (1976): 27-37, 159-169.

Mahar, Margaret. "Hardy's Poetry of Renunciation." *English Literary History* 45 (1978): 303-324.

Millgate, Michael. *Thomas Hardy: A Biography*. New York: Random House, 1982.

Southerington, F. R. "Thomas Hardy in *Jude the Obscure*." *The Thomas Hardy Yearbook* 1 (1970): 62-69.

Alden, Patricia. "A Short Story Prelude to *Jude the Obscure*: More Light on the Genesis of Hardy's Last Novel." *The Colby Library Quarterly* 19.1 (1983): 45-52.

Alden comments upon the existence of a short story by Hardy published prior to the novel *Jude the Obscure*. She believes that one of the major themes in the novel *Jude* was first expressed in the short story identified as "A Tragedy of Two Ambitions." The theme she focuses on is that of "frustrated academic ambitions" (46). Alden states, "Both story and novel take seriously the situation of the intelligent, industrious, scholarly poor man barred from the prestigious university he aspires to enter" (48). She continues her discussion by comparing the two works in terms of plot description and character analysis. Specifically, Alden examines the actions and the motives of Jude (*Jude*

the Obscure) and Joshua and Cornelius ("Tragedy of Two Ambitions").
The overall premise of the article is interesting, and Alden's arguments
seem plausible.

Casagrande, Peter J. " 'Something More to be Said': Hardy's Creative
   Process and the Case of *Tess* and *Jude*." *New Perspectives on
   Thomas Hardy*. Ed. Charles Pettit. New York: St. Martin's Press,
   1994. 16-40.
Casagrande divides his article into four distinct sections. In the
introductory portion of the article, Casagrande discusses three phases of
Hardy's development as a writer. Next, he goes on to describe Hardy's
own views about writing and to explain how these ideas influenced
Hardy's own creative processes. After some additional background
information in Section I and setting the historical context in Section II,
Casagrande goes on to discuss the reading of two novels in particular.
He suggests that *Tess of the d'Urbervilles* and *Jude the Obscure* be read
consecutively and examined critically simultaneously. Casagrande
views *Jude* as something like an extension of *Tess*. He states:

> In *Jude* Hardy transmuted his story of the neglected, sexually violated
> peasant girl into the story of an orphaned, sexually victimized boy of the
> rural working classes. (29)

Casagrande goes on to point out many similarities that exist within the
two stories. He provides a general summary of each of the novels and
interjects critical comments throughout each portion of the article.
Casagrande concludes by pointing out that while some significant
differences do exist between Tess's story and Jude's, the similarities are
too numerous to be ignored. In general, the article is interesting, and it
is organized logically. It provides useful information for readers who
wish to explore Hardy's views on writing and who are interested in
examining both the novels *Tess of the d'Urbervilles* and *Jude the
Obscure*.

Greenslade, William. "Edward Carpenter on *Jude the Obscure*: An
   Unpublished Letter." *English Language Notes* 24.3 (1987): 37-38.
In this short selection, Greenslade discusses the existence of a letter
written by one of Hardy's contemporaries, Socialist writer Edward
Carpenter. The letter records Carpenter's praise of *Jude the Obscure*.
This is significant because Carpenter's positive comments were at
variance with much of the criticism written at the time of the novel's

initial publication. Carpenter specifically praises Hardy's "clear treatment of female sexuality" (38).

Ingham, Patricia. "The Evolution of *Jude the Obscure*." *The Review of English Studies* 27 (1976): 27-37, 159-169.

Ingham's discussion centers on the existing manuscript of the novel. She describes the publication history of *Jude the Obscure* and provides explanations regarding the various versions of the novel both in serial and book form. In addition, Ingham includes examples of correspondence between Hardy and his publisher, J. Henry Harper, that may serve to explain certain changes that took place in the manuscript prior to its publication. In the latter half of the article, Ingham discusses the evolution of the themes of marriage and academic ambition. Also, Ingham identifies possible sources of inspiration for Hardy, such as the death of his niece/cousin Tryphena Sparks or his visit to Oxford in the summer of 1893. In describing how she believes the novel took shape, Ingham notes that evidence from the manuscript indicates

> that the schoolmaster Phillotson evidently did not exist when the first eighty-four pages of the manuscript were written, since the references before that point are all additions or alterations. (161)

Ingham refers to alterations in Sue's characterization and circumstance as well. As a result of her careful study, Ingham provides readers with many insights regarding the development of the novel. She presents the information in a well-organized and accessible format.

Southerington, F. R. "Thomas Hardy in *Jude the Obscure*." *The Thomas Hardy Yearbook* 1 (1970): 62-69.

In this brief article, Southerington discusses the possible links between the novel *Jude the Obscure* and Hardy's own life. Southerington describes the similarities between the character Jude and Thomas Hardy himself. In referring to Jude Fawley and Hardy, Southerington states, "Both are deeply sensitive to the pain and suffering in nature. Both begin life as shy, frail children. Both experience the wish not to grow up. . . ." (63). In addition to discussing the personality traits of Jude and Hardy, Southerington compares the events in Hardy's life with the events in Jude's. Many incidents from the novel are examined, as are the relationships that Jude forms with the other characters. Much information about Hardy's relationships with his mother, paternal grandmother, and cousin Tryphena Sparks is presented. In general, Southerington's remarks are intriguing, but some of the evidence he provides is of a speculative nature.

Comparative Studies

Findlay, L. M. "D. G. Rossetti and *Jude the Obscure*." *The Pre-Raphaelite Review* 2.1 (1978): 1-11.

Findlay attempts to establish a link between Hardy's novel, *Jude the Obscure*, and the poems and paintings of D. G. Rossetti. Findlay agrees that the "barrier theme" (3) is present in the works of both Hardy and Rossetti. Also, Findlay lists and describes a number of Rossetti's paintings that seem to possess qualities similar to those expressed in Hardy's novel *Jude the Obscure*. Included in the article are descriptions of several significant scenes from the novel in addition to the descriptions of Rossetti's artwork. Findlay concludes by saying, "What seems to be happening is that Hardy adopts an idiom to which Rossetti had already contributed generously as both a poet and a painter" (7).

Gemmette, Elizabeth Villiers. "G. Eliot's *Mill on the Floss* and Hardy's *Jude the Obscure*." *The Explicator* 42.3 (1984): 28-30.

Gemmette essentially examines the similarities between the actions of Maggie Tulliver (*Mill on the Floss*) and Sue Bridehead (*Jude the Obscure*). She states, "A definite identifiable need appears to motivate both Maggie and Sue: the need to be loved" (28). Gemmette goes on to compare Maggie's relationship with Tom in comparison to Sue's relationship with Jude. Although the article is brief, Gemmette raises some interesting points. However, a knowledge of both novels is essential to a clear understanding of her views.

Mohan, Devinder. "Romanticism and the Woman: A Comparative View of Hawthorne's Hester Prynne, Hardy's Sue Bridehead, Chatterjee's Rohini and Hesse's Kamala." *The Literary Half-Yearly* 27.1 (1986): 78-88.

Mohan opens the article with a discussion of the theme of "the natural affinity between woman's sexuality and love for man and in turn, man's awe and admiration in reciprocating the same . . ." (78). Mohan goes on to specifically describe the situations faced by Hester Prynne, Sue Bridehead, Rohini, and Kamala in terms of the rules placed on them by society. Mohan identifies similarities in their development as characters as well as in the obstacles they face as women in male-dominated societies.

Nemesvari, Richard. "Appropriating the Word: *Jude the Obscure* as Subversive Apocrypha." *Victorian Review* 19.2 (1993): 48-66.

In this somewhat challenging article, Nemesvari identifies and describes possible links between elements of *Jude the Obscure* and some of the apocryphal writings associated with the Bible. Nemesvari specifically identifies the story of Susanna that was at one time included at the end of the book of Daniel as a possible as well as probable source of inspiration for Hardy. In terms of the canonized books of the Bible, Nemesvari cites the book of Jude as having a significant relationship to Hardy's text. Nemesvari also describes Hardy's use of various scriptural allusions throughout the novel and asserts that he did so in a way that creates a reversal of the more traditional value system of the period. Further, he argues that Sue and Jude's relationship is based on an alternate set of principles unlike those governing legal marriage. Nemesvari states that the "advancement of love as the legitimizing factor in human relationships, as opposed to the letter of the law, is the novel's central tenet" (63). He then continues by discussing Hardy's possible reasons for so challenging the conventions of the age. Overall, the article is very informative and provides readers with unique insights regarding the development of the central ideas presented in the novel.

Pickrel, Paul. "*Jude the Obscure* and the Fall of Phaethon." *Hudson Review* (1986): 231-250.

Pickrel examines the responses of male readers to *Jude the Obscure*. He refers to the work of Robert May, whose book *Sex and Fantasy* seems to provide a psychological basis for the male reader's response to the novel. Later in the article, Pickrel explains how Jude's story relates to the story of Phaethon. He states, "Clearly *Jude the Obscure* tells a story of the same general type as the Phaethon myth: a youth of high ambition seeks to follow a noble course and fails" (236). Then, Pickrel goes on to describe aspects of Sue's and Jude's characters that are similar to the characteristics evident in the young Phaethon. He also discusses the various patterns that Hardy developed throughout the novel in terms of the characters as well as the plot. Pickrel concludes his discussion by pointing out additional elements of the novel, such as the presence of Arabella and Sue, that he feels are part of its overall appeal. Although several of Pickrel's comments seem of a speculative nature, he does make some interesting points. In general, the piece is well organized and not difficult to read.

Renner, Stanley. "Mary Teller and Sue Bridehead: Birds of a Feather in 'The White Quail' and *Jude the Obscure*." *Steinbeck Quarterly* 18.1-2 (1985): 35-45.

Renner discusses Steinbeck's knowledge of Hardy's works and the possibility that Steinbeck may have been directly influenced by his reading of Hardy's novels, specifically *The Return of the Native* and *Jude the Obscure*. Renner then goes on to describe the similarities that exist between the characters Sue Bridehead (*Jude*) and Mary Teller ("The White Quail"). Renner observes that "Mary Teller and Sue Bridehead are uncannily alike—in detailed resemblance, in attitude, and in the havoc they wreak in their relationships with men" (36). He goes on to identify and describe the physical characteristics of the two women as well as the emotional/spiritual aspects of their nature. Later, Renner identifies a number of parallels between the two stories in terms of plot development as well as theme. Renner makes a number of interesting observations and provides a number of examples from each text to support his claims.

Nature of the Novel

Draper, Ronald P. "Hardy's Comic Tragedy: *Jude the Obscure*." Critical Essays on British Literature. *Critical Essays on Thomas Hardy: The Novels*. Eds. Dale Kramer and Nancy Marck. Boston: G. K. Hall, 1990. 243-254.

Draper describes two contrasting pictures in the novel *Jude the Obscure*. He identifies both tragic and comic elements from within the text of the novel and briefly discusses its plot. Then, Draper turns to a discussion regarding the relationships of the three principal characters Jude, Sue, and Arabella. In discussing their various characteristics, he states:

> Sue and Arabella can also be seen as the embodiments of the Spirit and the Flesh respectively, which, failing to cohere in the same woman, split Jude so that he becomes dangerously divided against himself. (252)

Throughout the remainder of the article, Draper returns to his discussion of the tragi-comic nature of the novel. He argues that the contrasting features of the characters as well as the plot make it difficult to define the novel within the restrictions of a single term. He concludes by arguing that the novel is a mixture of the "tragical-comical-historical-antipastoral-satirical, and even parodic . . ." (254). However, Draper expresses his admiration for the novel in spite of its curious mixture of contrasting elements.

Prentiss, Norman D. "The Tortured Form of *Jude the Obscure.*" *Colby Quarterly* 31.3 (1995): 179-193.

Prentiss argues that the form of the novel *Jude the Obscure* is cyclical in nature. Early in the article, he states:

> The cycle of events that gives the novel its shape results in the characters' suffering and humiliation; the final section of the novel is only the culmination of a continuing series of painful repetitions. (180)

He continues by describing how the major characters are unable to progress or move forward even though they move from place to place throughout the novel. Prentiss provides numerous examples from the text to support his claims. He also discusses the actions of Sue, Jude, Arabella, Phillotson, and Little Father Time in some detail. In the concluding portion of the article, he argues that the novel is "about the failure of language" (193) and is Hardy's response to the difficulty of creating a narrative that complies with the conventions of the traditional narrative form.

Pyle, Forest. "Demands of History: Narrative Crisis in *Jude the Obscure.*" *New Literary History* 26.2 (1995): 359-378.

Pyle divides his somewhat lengthy article into several sections. He begins by discussing Hardy's interest in time and history. He asserts that, in general, the body of

> Hardy's work is an allegory of the confrontations between the historicizing impulse and the textual resistances posed by the narrative medium through which history is to be conveyed. (360)

Later, Pyle describes aspects of *Jude the Obscure* that demonstrate Hardy's attempts to represent history through description rather than narration. In the portion of the article subtitled "Monuments of History,

Sites of Time," Pyle discusses Hardy's use of spatial organization to convey a sense of the archaeological past, and he goes on in the following section to assert that "Hardy conceived of the organization of *Jude the Obscure* in spatial terms" (373). In general, Pyle's discussion of the novel is interesting and thought provoking; however, the complicated nature of his discussions may prove problematic for the general reader.

Salient Features of the Novel

Beckingham, Cushla R. "The Importance of Family in Hardy's Fictional World." *The Thomas Hardy Journal* 5.2 (1985): 62-68.

Beckingham's article provides a brief discussion of Hardy's views regarding the importance of heredity as they are addressed in his poetry and in his novels. A variety of Victorian ideologies are discussed and examples of the ways in which these ideologies are reflected in Hardy's works are provided. Beckingham focuses on "familism" as an environmental force which exerts pressure on the individual but points out that Hardy's view of heredity was, like his views of other forces, a response to what he read and believed, rather than consistent exposition or elucidation of the science of heredity itself (64). Also included in the article are several specific examples of Hardy's views as they relate to the text of *Jude the Obscure*. Overall, the article is successful in its attempt to address issues relating to the significance of family in Hardy's works.

Cline, Ralph M., and Eleanor C. Guetzloe. "*Jude the Obscure*: A Pathway to Suicide." Y*outh Suicide Prevention: Lessons from Literature*. Eds. Sara Munson and Lagretta Tallent Lenken. New York: Insight Books, 1989. 115-134.

Cline and Guetzloe begin the chapter with a general discussion of the plot of the novel *Jude the Obscure*. Then they provide some background information relating to the initial publication of the novel as well as its early critical reception. Next, Cline and Guetzloe discuss the suicidal tendencies evident in Jude and Father Time as well as the incidents with which the two characters are involved. They also bring in data relating to current suicide trends and assert that "some of the specific problems discussed by Thomas Hardy are current as well as historic" (133). Cline and Guetzloe close by arguing that some of the risk factors present in the novel can be identified today and further that an identification of the factors in literature or in life is the first step to solving the problem of youth suicide.

Dellamora, Richard. "Male Relations in Thomas Hardy's *Jude the Obscure.*" *Papers on Language and Literature* 27.4 (1991): 453-472.
Dellamora primarily examines the relationships between Jude and the other male figures in the novel while also investigating the prevailing attitude towards male relationships during the Victorian period. In addition, Dellamora describes Jude's relationship with Sue and the effects it produces upon their lives. In describing how the other characters in the novel view their relationship, he states: "Jude's acquaintances among upwardly mobile working class regard his sexual nonconformity as a slur on their respectability . . ." (458). As a result, Jude is isolated from his male counterparts and ultimately excluded from the professional society to which he belonged while at Aldbrickham. To further support his assertions regarding the type of relationships that were deemed acceptable during the Victorian period, Dellamora distinguishes between the ambitious desires of men and the erotic desires of men. He provides examples from the text that seem to illustrate one or both types of desire and explains how Hardy's personal experiences with Horace Moule may have influenced his treatment of such matters within the text of the novel.

Fischler, Alexander. "An Affinity for Birds: Kindness in Hardy's *Jude the Obscure.*" *Studies in the Novel* 13.3 (1981): 250-265.
In his somewhat unusual approach to a discussion of *Jude the Obscure*, Fischler describes the significance of birds and references to birds throughout the novel. He opens the article by describing Phillotson's remarks to the young Jude about treating birds and animals with kindness. He goes on to discuss a number of the heroines portrayed by Hardy, but states that "Until we meet Sue Bridehead, we have little to mark the evolution of a specific type which might be called the bird bride" (254). In the remaining portion of the article, Fischler explores Sue's, Jude's, and Arabella's relationships with one another while continually referring to Jude's acts of kindness towards each of the two women. He reaffirms his assertion relating to the overall significance of the bird motif and describes how Jude's kindness works against him. Finally, included within the article are bits of information

regarding Hardy's sources of inspiration for the novel as well as references to aspects of the composition and publication processes.

Fischler, Alexander. "A Kinship with Job: Obscurity and Remembrance in Hardy's *Jude the Obscure*." *Journal of English and Germanic Philology* 84.4 (1985): 515-533.

Fischler begins his article by discussing the presence of five themes within the novel. He identifies the themes of obscurity and remembrance as being significant and then describes how the two themes are present in Jude's story as well as in Job's. He states that "By recalling repeatedly the story of Job, a potentially overwhelming backdrop, Hardy universalized Jude's plot" (516). Fischler goes on to describe, in some detail, Jude's experiences throughout the novel. He points to many areas in which Jude's experiences parallel those of Job and provides numerous examples from the text to support his claims. Fischler also presents information relating to Hardy's other possible sources of inspiration or motivation and identifies a number of Biblical and literary allusions other than those which refer specifically to Job. In general, the article provides readers with a wealth of information and is well organized in its presentation of the material.

Freeman, Janet H. "Highways and Cornfields: Space and Time in the Narration of *Jude the Obscure*." *Colby Quarterly* 27.3 (1991): 161-173.

Freeman addresses the three aspects of space, time, and narration in *Jude the Obscure*. She begins by describing Jude's various travels from one place to another throughout the novel. Next, Freeman provides numerous examples of how the constraints of time affect the lives of Jude and Sue. In referring specifically to Jude's notion of time, she states that his

> conception of time stretched out in linear fashion like the roads and railway lines he follows to get from one place to another or the intellectual progress he hopes to make. (166)

However, Freeman would argue that Hardy's conception of time is different from Jude's. She asserts that Hardy takes a great deal of care in his narrative to present time as an accumulation of events which cannot be ignored or forgotten. Freeman presents her arguments in a clear and original fashion, and the three aspects that she has chosen to address represent topics of interest to the general as well as the scholarly reader.

Giordano, Frank R. "Secularization and Ethical Authority in *Jude the Obscure*." *The Thomas Hardy Yearbook* 3 (1972-1973): 34-40.

Giordano discusses the ways in which "Thomas Hardy's final novel, *Jude the Obscure*, illustrates quite clearly the decay and degradation that mark the decline of religion in modern times" (34). Throughout the article, he traces the moves of the major characters away from the established codes of religion toward a more secularized view of life. Giordano also describes "the elimination of religious symbols from the landscape" as outlined in the novel (36). In addition, he identifies and describes what he feels is one of the major themes present in the novel, that of the severe adherence to the letter of the law. In this brief article, Giordano makes a variety of interesting observations regarding aspects of the plot, setting, and character development. His ideas are logically organized and clearly presented.

Goetz, William R. "The Felicity and Infelicity of Marriage in *Jude the Obscure*." *Nineteenth-Century Fiction* 38.2 (1983): 189-213.

Goetz begins by describing the significance of the marriage theme in *Jude the Obscure*. He discusses Hardy's own remarks regarding its importance in the novel and makes the observation that "Marriage finds its place in this tragedy, not only as a social theme but as an institution whose form lends itself to the shape of the novel Hardy is trying to write" (192). Goetz then discusses the nature of the marriage contract in terms of its language and meaning. He also addresses the existence of marriage laws and explains how the various principal characters enter into their marriage arguments. Goetz provides numerous details from the text to support his arguments, and although the article is somewhat lengthy, the information is well organized and accessible to readers.

Hagen, June Steffensen. "Does Teaching Make a Difference in Ethical Reflection?: A Report on Teaching Hardy's *Jude the Obscure* with Attention to Marriage, Divorce, and Remarriage." *Christianity and Literature* 33.3 (1984): 23-35.

Hagen essentially relates the results of a study she conducted regarding student responses to the teaching of the novel *Jude the Obscure*. Although the survey she administered includes over 70 questions, Hagen presents the following question as the focal point for her study. She asks:

> Does my teaching of Thomas Hardy's novel *Jude the Obscure* affect student opinion on an ethical issue, in this case, divorce and remarriage, and if so, in what direction does it do so? (24)

The results of her survey are interesting, particularly to those who have the opportunity to teach. The data gained from Hagen's study are presented in a logical fashion, and a copy of the student questionnaire is included at the conclusion of the article.

Henigan, Julie. "Hardy's Emblem of Futility: The Role of Christminster in *Jude the Obscure*." *The Thomas Hardy Yearbook* 14 (1987): 12-14.

In this brief article, Henigan primarily discusses Jude's relationship with Christminster and his repeated attempts to belong to its society of scholars. She argues that while "Christminster dominates Jude's life, it is Jude himself, however, who gives it the power to do so" (14). She further argues that the choices Jude makes throughout the novel contribute as much to his failure as do the circumstances of fate or the pressures created by society. She concludes her discussion by stating that the central message of the novel is one that recognizes the futility of human life but also one that recognizes the individual's contribution to that futility.

Mahar, Margaret. "Hardy's Poetry of Renunciation." *English Literary History* 45 (1978): 303-324.

Although Mahar's article primarily focuses on an analysis of Hardy's poetry, she opens her discussion with comments relating to the novel *Jude the Obscure*. She observes that

> *Jude the Obscure*, and perhaps all of Hardy's novels, are self-conscious regarding their inability to rationalize the cause and effect of tragedy or join past and present within a credible organic whole. (304)

Mahar also describes Hardy's move from novel writing to the writing of poetry. Throughout her analysis of the poetry, she refers to the differences between the form of a novel and the form of poetry and argues that by the time Hardy was writing *Jude the Obscure*, he felt restricted by such constraints as having to continually recreate an

Aristotelean plot. She says, "In the lyric poem, Hardy found his freedom" (305). To support this assertion, she discusses several poems in some detail and identifies many of the poetic devices used by Hardy. Mahar's observations are intriguing, and this article aids readers in their understanding of the novel *Jude the Obscure* as well as a select body of Hardy's poems.

McCormack, Peggy A. "The Syntax of Quest in *Jude the Obscure*." *The New Orleans Review* 8.1 (1981): 42-48.

To support her argument that unity of theme and imagery exists in the novel *Jude the Obscure*, McCormack examines the plot of the novel in terms of its syntactical construction. She centers her discussion on what she identifies as the quest episodes. In referring to the actions of Jude, Arabella, and Phillotson, she states that the "characters seek goals and are blocked or facilitated in reaching these goals by natural and societal forces" (42). McCormack goes on to specifically identify Jude's goals as they exist at the beginning of the novel. She argues that "Jude's goals—education, spirituality and human love—are ideal and cultural to his mind" (42). Further, she explains that as Jude's pursuit of these goals is thwarted by various blocking agents, he attempts to substitute one goal for another. Somewhat later in the article, McCormack explains her view that the novel itself can be divided into two sections. The first half, she asserts, is devoted primarily to Jude's quests while in the second half of the novel Arabella and Phillotson begin their quest to destroy the union of Sue and Jude. McCormack concludes her essay with a chart illustrating the syntactical pattern of each of the previously described quests. The pattern she suggests, in both halves of the novel, is subject—action—direct object—modifiers of the action. Although McCormack's approach to the novel is somewhat unusual, her discussion helps readers to better understand the nature of the plot as well as the actions of the characters.

McNees, Eleanor. "Reverse Typology in *Jude the Obscure*." *Christianity and Literature* 39.1 (1989): 35-49.

McNees explores the ways in which Hardy's religious beliefs are manifested throughout the novel *Jude the Obscure*. She explains how the traditional typology of fulfillment after conversion is not carried out in the novel. McNees states:

As Jude journeys from New Testament antitype (St. Jude, Christ, even Judas) to Old Testament type (Samson, Job), he demonstrates the extinction of the spirit by the letter and thus reverses the order of Paul's advice to the Corinthians. (39)

Then, McNees describes in some detail the various decisions Jude makes throughout his life. She discusses Hardy's use of Biblical allusions, arguing that "The Biblical allusions hasten the progression of the plot towards its negative fulfillment" (42). To support her assertions, McNees frequently refers to the works of numerous critics. The overall premise of the article is interesting and the material is presented in a logical manner.

Wasserman, Julian N. "A Note on the Church of St. Thomas in *Jude the Obscure.*" *The Thomas Hardy Yearbook* 14 (1987): 9-12.

This brief but interesting article points out the significance of Hardy's specific reference to the church known as Sarum St. Thomas in *Jude the Obscure*. Wasserman argues that if Hardy were merely trying to establish a certain mood, the exactness of the reference would be unnecessary. However, Wasserman asserts that the church Hardy does mention would have been well known to many of his readers because of an important feature within its interior. Inside the church is a famous painting called the Doom Portrait. In the portrait, Christ is shown in the Heavenly Jerusalem. On one side of the Christ figure the saints are shown rising to the city; on the other side of the figure those who are damned are shown falling into Hell. Wasserman relates the scene depicted in the portrait to Jude's experience at Christminster. He states:

> Thus, the disparity between the Jerusalem that appears in the Chancel portrait and the heavenly city of the young man's fantasies is as real and thematically significant as the Christminster of fact and the mythical romanticized city that is the focal point of the would-be scholar's aspirations. (11)

Wasserman concludes by noting that very few scholars have made reference to Hardy's or his contemporaries' probable knowledge of the Doom Portrait and in doing so have neglected an intriguing aspect of the novel *Jude the Obscure*.

Character Analysis

Dawson, E. W. "Two 'Flat' Characters in *Jude the Obscure.*" *The Lock Haven Review* 6 (1964): 36-44.

   Dawson centers his discussion on the plausibility of the actions of Father Time and Vilbert as well as their effectiveness as characters. He refers to the work of E. M. Forster, *Aspects of the Novel*, for definitions of flat and round characters. He asserts that Father Time is basically a flat character that ultimately fails to be convincing in his thoughts or actions. Dawson goes on to describe the events that lead up to the deaths of the children and states, "The triple hanging is simply the crowning surprise in a series of increasingly unconvincing surprises" (39). In the next section of the article, he turns the discussion to Vilbert. Although Dawson views Vilbert as an essentially flat character also, he feels that Hardy's treatment of Vilbert is consistent and convincing. In closing, Dawson argues against those who, in general, view the novel as a failure. He states that he feels that the intensity of action is maintained even to the novel's conclusion.

Edwards, Suzanne. "A Shadow from the Past: Little Father Time in *Jude the Obscure.*" *The Colby Library Quarterly* 23.1 (1987): 32-38.

   Edwards examines aspects of the role of Little Father Time, arguing that "he appropriately functions to advance the plot and to symbolize the mistakes Jude has made in the past" (32). She goes on to describe the similarities between Jude and his son in terms of their behaviors and attitudes. Edwards points out that both characters express their personal wish that they had not been born. She states, "When manifested in his son, Jude's misfortunes and weaknesses become exaggerated" (36). To support this assertion, Edwards provides a series of examples from the text of the novel but stresses the significance of the hanging incident. Her ideas are clearly expressed and are presented in an organized and logical manner.

Gordon, Jan B. "Gossip and the Letter: Ideologies of 'Restoration' in *Jude the Obscure.*" *Love and Language* 8.1 (1989): 45-48

   Gordon begins this brief discussion by focusing on the characters Father Time and Vilbert. Gordon argues that

> In their own separate ways, Father Time and Vilbert are emblems of the attempted recuperation of history: one at home nowhere; the other, at home virtually anywhere. (46)

Gordon goes on to describe how characters like Jude, Sue, Phillotson, and Arabella each attempt a series of new beginnings as a way toward restoration of the past. Later in the article is a discussion regarding the nature of gossip as "an agent of the recovery of knowledge" (48). Although this selection is short, the arguments are somewhat difficult to follow, and the material is presented in a disjointed fashion.

Kelley, Mary Ann. "Individuation and Consummation in Hardy's *Jude the Obscure.*" *The Victorian Newsletter* 82 (1992): 62-64.
   Kelley's discussion centers on the analysis of Jude's actions as they relate to the ideas expressed in the works of Arthur Schopenhauer. She describes Jude's need to belong and his search for fulfillment

> as a dramatization of Schopenhauer's irrational and impulsive Will to live: incessantly seeking contentment through connection but more often finding pain in thwarted connections. (62)

Kelley continues her discussion by including examples from the text of the novel and by explaining how Hardy's knowledge of and interest in Schopenhauer's ideas may have influenced his portrayal of Jude as well as his development of the story line. Kelley's ideas are clearly and succinctly presented, and her arguments are intriguing.

LeVay, John. "Hardy's *Jude the Obscure.*" *The Explicator* 49.4 (1991): 219-222.
   In this brief selection LeVay links the four major characters, Jude, Sue, Arabella, and Phillotson, to the four elements of fire, air, earth, and water, respectively. He provides a series of short descriptions and examples from the text of the novel to support his assertion that the four elements are represented by the four characters. His observations are unique and offer readers some interesting insights into the traits of the major characters in the novel.

Mallett, Phillip. "Sexual Ideology and Narrative Form in *Jude the Obscure.*" *English* 162 (1989): 211-224.
   Mallett begins his article by examining the views of previous critics relating to the character Sue Bridehead. He goes on to state his view

that "The narrative form of the novel is organized to show how Sue is taught to see herself first of all as a woman, second as Sue Bridehead/Phillotson/Fawley, and finally again as a woman . . ." (212). Next, Mallett presents background information regarding marriage laws as well as the conventional marriage practices of the period. Further, he identifies aspects of the text that reveal how the narrator's views on marriage are reflected within the text of the novel. Somewhat later, Mallett provides numerous examples of Hardy's use of literary and Biblical allusion and concludes by reiterating his assertion that Sue's plight is the centralizing force in the structure of the novel.

Simpson, Anne B. "Sue Bridehead Revisited." *Victorian Literature and Culture* 19 (1991): 55-66.

Simpson primarily addresses the problem critics and scholars have encountered when trying to classify Sue as a specific type of character. She describes various contrasting aspects present in Sue's character and argues that Sue "resists categorization" (56). To support her claims, Simpson also provides a number of examples from the text of the novel. Simpson states that "Sue offers a stimulating critique of the assumption that a definable femininity can be grasped through rigorous investigation by either writer or reader" (64). In general, Simpson's comments are intriguing; however, her discussion demands some prior knowledge of the content and scope of previous criticism, and, as a result, may prove somewhat challenging to the general reader.

Watts, Cedric. "Hardy's Sue Bridehead and the 'New Woman.' " *Critical Survey* 5.2 (1993): 152-156.

Watts examines Hardy's claims in the postscript added to the 1895 preface to *Jude the Obscure* where Hardy describes the reaction of a German reviewer toward the serial version of the novel. The reviewer specifically praised Hardy's depiction of Sue as a new type of woman. The reviewer also recognizes Hardy as the first to delineate such a character. Watts then goes on to describe various historical incidents that reveal changes in women's roles during the time prior to the novel's publication. Watts also provides examples of other pieces of writing that address issues similar to those addressed in *Jude*, and which include characters whose traits are similar to Sue's. However, Watt concludes the article by stating:

When *Jude the Obscure* is compared with other novels of that time which depict the New Woman, Hardy's novel is more vivid, intense and moving than they are. (156)

Overall, the article is very informative and provides readers with insights regarding the development of Sue's character.

Appendix A
Computer Connections

There are a variety of sources relating to Thomas Hardy that can be obtained from the National Trust Office located in Dorchester as well as the Dorset County Museum. In addition to pamphlets, books, and recordings generally available both in the United States and in England, it should be noted that a number of catalogs for the secondary education/university instructor include various teaching aids relating to the life and works of Thomas Hardy. Also listed in these catalogs are a wide range of software application packages, including a variety of CD-ROM products. There is a wide range of information available on the Internet; however, it is important for Internet users to recognize that, at this point, the sources available on the Net may not necessarily be authentic or accurate. Those who access the Thomas Hardy web site should be aware that the information presented at this site is not, at this time, recognized or sanctioned by any particular scholarly group or members of The Thomas Hardy Society.

Appendix B
Works Cited

Adamson, Jane. "Tess, Time, and Its Shapings." *The Critical Review* 26 (1984): 18-36.

Adey, Lionel. "Styles of Love in *Far from the Madding Crowd*." *Thomas Hardy Annual* 5 (1987): 47-62.

Alden, Patricia. "A Short Story Prelude to *Jude the Obscure*: More Light on the Genesis of Hardy's Last Novel." *The Colby Library Quarterly* 19.1 (1983): 45-52.

Altick, Richard. *Victorian People and Ideas*. New York: W. W. Norton & Company, 1973.

Arkans, Norman. "Hardy's Novel Impression—Pictures." *The Colby Library Quarterly* 22.3 (1986): 153-164.

Aschkenasy, Nehama. "Biblical Substructures in the Tragic Form: Hardy, *The Mayor of Casterbridge*, and Agnon, *And the Crooked Shall Be Made Straight*." *Modern Language Studies* 13.1 (1983): 101-110.

Atkins, N. F. *Hardy, Tess and Myself*. Beaminster: The Toucan Press, 1962.

Atkinson, F. G. "The Inevitable Movement Onward—Some Aspects of *The Return of the Native*." *The Thomas Hardy Yearbook* 3 (1972): 10-17.

Babb, Howard. "Setting and Theme in *Far from the Madding Crowd*." *English Literary History* 30 (1963): 147-161.

Baily, J. O. *The Poetry of Thomas Hardy: A Handbook and Commentary*. Chapel Hill: University of North Carolina Press, 1970.

Bair, Judith. "*The Mayor of Casterbridge*: 'Some Grand Feat of Stagery.' " *South Atlantic Bulletin* 42.2 (1977): 11-22.

Baldridge, Cates. "Observation and Domination in Hardy's *The Woodlanders*." *Victorian Literature and Culture* 21 (1993): 193-209.

Ball, David. "Tragic Contradiction in Hardy's *The Woodlanders*. ARIEL: *A Review of International English Literature* 18.1 (1987): 17-25.

Barber, D. F., ed. *Concerning Thomas Hardy*. London: Charles Skilton, Ltd., 1968.

Bayley, John. "A Social Comedy? On Re-reading *The Woodlanders*." *Thomas Hardy Annual* 5 (1987): 3-21.

Beach, Joseph Warren. *The Technique of Thomas Hardy*. New York: Russell and Russell, 1962.

Beatty, C. J. P. "Thomas Hardy and Thomas Hughes." *English Studies* 68 (1987): 511-518.

Bebbington, Brian. "Folksong and Dance in *The Mayor of Casterbridge*." *English Dance and Song* 40 (1978): 111-115.

Beckingham, Cushla R. "The Importance of Family in Hardy's Fictional World." *The Thomas Hardy Journal* 5.2 (1985) : 62-68.

Beegel, Susan. "Bathsheba's Lovers: Male Sexuality in *Far from the Madding Crowd*." *Tennessee Studies in Literature* 27 (1984): 108-127.

Beningfield, Gordon, and Anthea Zeman. *Hardy Country*. London: Allen Lane, 1983.

Benway, Ann M. Baribault. "Oedipus Abroad: Hardy's Clym Yeobright and Lawrence's Paul Morel." *The Thomas Hardy Yearbook* 13 (1986): 51-57.

Bjork, Lennart A. " 'Visible Essences' as Thematic Structure in Hardy's *The Return of the Native.*" *English Studies* 53 (1972): 52-63.

Blank, Paula C. "*Tess of the d'Urbervilles*: The English Novel and the Foreign Plot." *Mid-Hudson Language Studies* 12 (1989): 62-71.

Boumelha, Penny. *Thomas Hardy and Women: Sexual Ideology and Narrative Form.* Sussex: Harvester Press, 1982.

Brasnett, Hugh. *Thomas Hardy: A Pictorial Guide.* Ringwood, Hampshire: Lodge Copse Press, 1990.

Buckler, William E. "Toward a Poetics of Hardy's Novels: *The Woodlanders.*" *Dickens Studies Annual* 14 (1985): 327-336.

Bullen, J. B. *The Expressive Eye: Fiction and Perception in the Work of Thomas Hardy.* Oxford: Clarendon Press, 1986.

— — —. "Thomas Hardy's *Far from the Madding Crowd*: Perception and Understanding." *The Thomas Hardy Journal* 3.2 (1987): 38-61.

Caless, Bryn. "The Nomenclature of Hardy's Novels: *The Mayor of Casterbridge.*" *The Thomas Hardy Yearbook* 5 (1975): 96-98.

Campbell, Elizabeth. "*Tess of the d'Urbervilles*: Misfortune Is a Woman." *The Victorian Newsletter* 76 (1989): 1-5.

Casagrande, Peter J. "A New View of Bathsheba Everdene." *Critical Approaches to the Novels of Thomas Hardy.* Ed. Dale Kramer. London: Macmillan, 1979. 50-73.

— — —. " 'The Shifted 'Center of Altruism' in *The Woodlanders*: Thomas Hardy's Third '*Return of the Native.*' " *English Literary History* 38 (1971): 104-125.

— — —. " 'Something More to be Said': Hardy's Creative Process and the Case of *Tess* and *Jude.*" *New Perspectives on Thomas Hardy.* Ed. Charles Pettit. New York: St. Martin's Press, 1994. 16-40.

— — —. *"Tess of the d'Urbervilles"*: *Unorthodox Beauty.* New York: Twayne, 1992.

Chalfront, Fran E. "From Strength to Strength: John Schlesinger's Film of *Far from the Madding Crowd.*" *Thomas Hardy Journal* 5 (1987): 63-74.

Chapman, Raymond. "The Reader as Listener: Dialect and Relationships in *The Mayor of Casterbridge.*" *The Pragmatics of Style.* Ed. Leo Hickey. London: Routledge, 1989. 159-178.

Chase, Mary Ellen. *Thomas Hardy from Serial to Novel.* New York: Russell & Russell, 1964.

Claridge, Laura. "Tess: A Less Than Pure Woman Ambivalently Presented." *Texas Studies in Literature and Language: A Journal of the Humanities* 28 (1986): 324-337.

Cline, Ralph M., and Eleanor C. Guetzloe. *"Jude the Obscure*: A Pathway to Suicide." *Youth Suicide Prevention: Lessons from Literature.* Eds. Sara Munson and Lagretta Tallent Lenker. New York: Insight Books, 1989. 115-134.

Cohen, Sandy. "Blind Clym, UnChristian and Christian and the Redness of the Reddleman: Character Correspondences in Hardy's *The Return of the Native.*" *The Thomas Hardy Yearbook* 11 (1984): 49-55.

Cooley, John R. "The Importance of Things Past: An Archetypal Reading of *The Mayor of Casterbridge.*" *Massachusetts Studies in English* 1 (1967): 17-21.

Corballis, Dr. Richard. "A Note on Mumming in *The Return of the Native.*" *The Thomas Hardy Yearbook* 5 (1975): 55-56.

Cornwell-Robinson, Margery. "Of Cows and Catfish: The Reading of Nature by Thomas Hardy and Loren Eiseley." *Soundings* 68 (1985): 52-61.

Cox, R. G., ed. *Thomas Hardy: The Critical Heritage.* New York: Barnes & Noble, Inc., 1970.

Cox, Stevens G. "Giles Symonds Alias *The Mayor of Casterbridge.*" *The Thomas Hardy Yearbook* 3 (1972-73): 24-26.

Cramer, Jeffrey S. "The Grotesque in Thomas Hardy's *The Woodlanders.*" *The Thomas Hardy Yearbook* 8 (1978): 25-29.

Davis, Karen. "A Deaf Ear to Essence: Music and Hardy's *The Mayor of Casterbridge.*" *Journal of English and German Philology* 89.2 (1990): 181-201.

Davis, William A. "'But he can be prosecuted for this': Legal and Sociological Backgrounds of the Mock Marriage in Hardy's Serial *Tess.*" *Colby Library Quarterly* 25.1 (1989): 28-41.

— — —. "Clough's 'Amours De Voyage' and Hardy's *The Return of the Native*: A Probable Source." *English Language Notes* 31.1 (1993): 47-55.

Dawson, E. W. "Two 'Flat' Characters in *Jude the Obscure.*" *The Lock Haven Review* 6 (1964): 36-44.

Dellamora, Richard. "Male Relations in Thomas Hardy's *Jude the Obscure.*" *Papers on Language and Literature* 27.4 (1991): 453-472.

Dollar, Gerard D. "Addiction and the 'Other Self' in Three Late Victorian Novels." *Beyond the Pleasure Dome: Writing and Addiction From the Romantics.* Ed. Tim Armstrong et al. Sheffield, England: Sheffield Academic Press, 1994. 268-274.

Draper, Ronald P. "Hardy's Comic Tragedy: *Jude the Obscure.*" Critical Essays on British Literature. In *Critical Essays on Thomas Hardy: The Novels.* Eds. Dale Kramer and Nancy Marck. Boston: G. K. Hall, 1990. 243-254.

— — —. "Introduction to the Case Book. Thomas Hardy: Three Pastoral Novels." *The Thomas Hardy Journal* 4.1 (1988): 36-49.

— — —. "*The Mayor of Casterbridge*." *Critical Quarterly* 25.1 (1983): 57-70.

— — —, and Phillip V. Mallett, eds. *A Spacious Vision: Essays on Hardy*. Newmill: Patten Press, 1994.

Easingwood, Peter. "*The Mayor of Casterbridge* and the Irony of Literary Production." *The Thomas Hardy Journal* 9.3 (1993): 64-75.

Eastman, Ronald. "Time and Propriety in *Far from the Madding Crowd*." *Interpretations* 10 (1978): 20-33.

Ebbatson, Roger. "The Plutonic Master: Hardy and the Steam Threshing-Machine." *Critical Survey* 2.1 (1989): 63-69.

Edwards, Anne-Marie. *In the Steps of Thomas Hardy*. Newbury, Berkshire: Countryside Books, 1989.

Edwards, Suzanne. "A Shadow from the Past: Little Father Time in *Jude the Obscure*." *The Colby Library Quarterly* 23.1 (1987): 32-38.

Egan, Joseph T. "The Indebtedness of George Douglas Brown to *The Mayor of Casterbridge*." *Studies in Scottish Literature* 27 (1992): 203-217.

Ellis, Reuben. "Joan Durbeyfield Writes to Margaret Saville: An Intermediary Reader in Thomas Hardy's *Tess of the d'Urbervilles*." *Colby Library Quarterly* 24.1 (1988): 14-26.

Epstein, Leonora. "Sale and Sacrament: The Wife Auction in *The Mayor of Casterbridge*." *English Language Notes* 24.4 (1987): 50-57.

Evans, Robert. "The Other Eustacia." *Novel* 1.3 (1968): 251-259.

Findlay, L. M. "An Affinity for Birds: Kindness in Hardy's *Jude the Obscure*." *Studies in the Novel* 13.3 (1981): 250-265.

— — —. "D. G. Rossetti and *Jude the Obscure*." *The Pre-Raphaelite Review* 2.1 (1978): 1-11.

Fischler, Alexander. "An Affinity for Birds: Kindness in Hardy's *Jude the Obscure*." *Studies in the Novel* 13.3 (1981): 250-265.

— — —. "A Kinship with Job: Obscurity and Remembrance in Hardy's *Jude the Obscure*." *Journal of English and Germanic Philology* 84.4 (1985): 515-533.

Fisher, Joe. *The Hidden Hardy*. New York: St. Martin's Press, 1992.

Fleissner, Robert F. "*Tess of the d'Urbervilles* and George Turberville." *Names* 37.1 (1989): 65-68.

Fontane, Marilyn Stall. "Hardy's Best Story." *The Thomas Hardy Yearbook* 11 (1984): 37-41.

Freeman, Janet. "Highways and Cornfields: Space and Time in the Narration of *Jude the Obscure*." *Colby Quarterly* 27.3 (1991): 161-173.

— — —. "Ways of Looking at *Tess*." *Studies in Philology* 79.3 (1982): 311-323.

Fussell, D. H. "The Maladroit Delay: The Changing Times in Hardy's *The Mayor of Casterbridge*." *Critical Quarterly* 21.3 (1979): 17-29.

Gadek, Lois Groner. "Tragic Potential and Narrative Perspective in Hardy's *The Return of the Native*." *The Thomas Hardy Yearbook* 14 (1987): 25-35.

Garson, Marjorie. *Hardy's Fables of Integrity*. Oxford: Clarendon Press, 1991.

Gatrell, Simon. "Angel Clare's Story." *The Thomas Hardy Journal* 7.3 (1991): 58-83.

— — —. "*Far from the Madding Crowd* Revisited." *The Thomas Hardy Journal* 10 (1994): 38-50.

— — —. *Hardy the Creator: A Textual Biography.* Oxford: Clarendon Press, 1988.

— — —. Introduction. *Far from the Madding Crowd.* By Thomas Hardy. New York: Oxford University Press, 1993. xiii-xxviii, xxx.

— — —. *Thomas Hardy and the Proper Study of Mankind.* Charlottesville: University Press of Virginia, 1993.

— — —, ed. *The Thomas Hardy Archive*: 2 (A Facsimile of the Manuscript with Related Materials). New York: Garland Publishing, 1986.

Gemmette, Elizabeth Villiers. "G. Eliot's *Mill on the Floss* and Hardy's *Jude the Obscure.*" *The Explicator* 42.3 (1984): 28-30.

Gerber, Helmut E., and W. Eugene Davis, eds. *Thomas Hardy: An Annotated Bibliography of Writings About Him.* DeKalb: Northern Illinois University Press, 1974.

Gibson, James. "*Tess of the d'Urbervilles.*" *The Thomas Hardy Journal* 7.3 (1991): 34-47.

Giordano, Frank R., Jr. *"I'd Have My Life Unbe": Thomas Hardy's Self-Destructive Characters.* Tuscaloosa, Alabama: University of Alabama Press, 1984.

— — —. "Secularization and Ethical Authority in *Jude the Obscure.*" *The Thomas Hardy Yearbook* 3 (1972-1973): 34-40.

Gittings, Robert. *Young Thomas Hardy: Thomas Hardy's Later Years.* New York: Quality Paperback Book Club, 1990.

Goetz, William R. "The Felicity and Infelicity of Marriage in *Jude the Obscure.*" *Nineteenth-Century Fiction* 38.2 (1983): 189-213.

Gordon, Jan B. "Gossip and the Letter: Ideologies of 'Restoration' in *Jude the Obscure.*" *Love and Language* 8.1 (1989): 45-48.

Goss, Michael. "Aspects of Time in *Far from the Madding Crowd.*" *The Thomas Hardy Journal* 6.3 (1990): 43-53.

Green, Brian. *Hardy's Lyrics: Pearls of Pity.* New York: St. Martin's Press, 1996.

Greenslade, William. "Edward Carpenter on *Jude the Obscure*: An Unpublished Letter." *English Language Notes* 24.3 (1987): 37-38.

— — —. "Hardy's 'Facts' Notebook: A Further Source for *The Mayor of Casterbridge.*" *The Thomas Hardy Journal* 2.1 (1986): 33-34.

— — —. "The Lure of Pedigree in *Tess of the d'Urbervilles.*" *The Thomas Hardy Journal* 7.3 (1991): 103-115.

Gregor, Ian. *The Great Web: The Form of Hardy's Major Fiction.* Totowa, New Jersey: Rowman and Littlefield, 1974.

Greiff, Louis K. "Symbolic Action in Hardy's *The Woodlanders*: An Application of Burkian Theory." *The Thomas Hardy Yearbook* 14 (1987): 52-62.

Grimsditch, Herbert B. *Character and Environment in the Novels of Thomas Hardy.* New York: Russell and Russell, 1922.

Grindle, Juliet M. "Compulsion and Choice in *The Mayor of Casterbridge.*" *The Novels of Thomas Hardy.* Ed. Anne Smith. New York: Barnes and Noble, 1979. 91-106.

Grinsell, Leslie. "Rainbarrows and Thomas Hardy." *The Thomas Hardy Journal* 2.2 (1986): 59-61.

Hagen, June Steffensen. "Does Teaching Make a Difference in Ethical Reflection?: A Report on Teaching Hardy's *Jude the Obscure* with Attention to Marriage, Divorce, and Remarriage." *Christianity and Literature* 33.3 (1984): 23-35.

Haig, Stirling. " 'By the Rivers of Babylon': Water and Exile in *The Mayor of Casterbridge.*" *The Thomas Hardy Yearbook* 11 (1984): 55-62.

Hands, Timothy. *A Hardy Chronology*. London: Macmillan, 1992.

— — —. *Thomas Hardy*. New York: St. Martin's Press, 1995.

— — —. *Thomas Hardy: Distracted Preacher*. New York: St. Martin's Press, 1989.

Hannaford, Richard. " 'A Forlorn Hope?' Grace Melbury and *The Woodlanders*." *The Thomas Hardy Yearbook* 10 (1980): 72-76.

— — —. "Ragnarok in Little Hintock: Norse Allusions in *The Woodlanders*." *The Thomas Hardy Yearbook* 6 (1976): 30-33.

Hardy, Thomas. *Far from the Madding Crowd*. Eds. Simon Gatrell and Suzanne B. Falck-Yi. New York: Oxford University Press, 1993.

— — —. *Jude the Obscure*. Eds. Simon Gatrell and Patricia Ingham. New York: Oxford University Press, 1985.

— — —. *The Life and Works of Thomas Hardy 1840-1928. 1928 and 1930*. Ed. Michael Millgate. Athens: University of Georgia Press, 1985.

— — —. *The Mayor of Casterbridge*. Eds. Simon Gatrell and Dale Kramer. New York: Oxford University Press, 1987.

— — —. *The Return of the Native*. Ed. Simon Gatrell. New York: Oxford University Press, 1990.

— — —. *Tess of the d'Urbervilles*. Eds. Simon Gatrell and Juliet Grindle. New York: Oxford University Press, 1988.

— — —. *The Woodlanders*. Eds. Simon Gatrell and Dale Kramer. New York: Oxford University Press, 1985.

"Hardy, Thomas." *The Oxford Companion to English Literature*. Ed. Margaret Drabble. New York: Oxford University Press, 1985.

— — —. *The Penguin Companion to English Literature*. Ed. David Daiches. New York: McGraw-Hill Book Company, 1971.

Hawkins, Desmond. "The Birds of Egdon Heath." *The Thomas Hardy Journal* 7.3 (1991): 86-87.

————. *Thomas Hardy: His Life and Landscape.* N. P.: The National Trust, 1990.

Henigan, Julie. "Hardy's Emblem of Futility: The Role of Christminster in *Jude the Obscure.*" *The Thomas Hardy Yearbook* 14 (1987): 12-14.

Higbie, Robert. "The Flight of the Swallow in *The Mayor of Casterbridge.*" *English Language Notes* 16.4 (1979): 311-312.

Higgins, Lesley. " 'Strange Webs of Melancholy': Shelleyan Echoes in *The Woodlanders.*" *Thomas Hardy Annual* 5 (1987): 38-46.

Higonnet, Margaret R. "Fictions of Feminine Voice: Antiphony and Silence in Hardy's *Tess of the d'Urbervilles.*" *Out of Bounds: Male Writers and Gender(ed) Criticism.* Ed. Laura Claridge. Amherst: University of Massachusetts Press, 1990. 197-218.

— — —, ed. *The Sense of Sex: Feminist Perspectives on Hardy.* Chicago: University of Illinois Press, 1993.

Holloway, John. *The Victorian Sage: Studies in Argument.* 1953. London: Macmillan, 1962.

Hornback, Bert G. *The Metaphor of Chance.* Athens: Ohio University Press, 1971.

Howe, Irving. *Thomas Hardy.* London: The Macmillan Co., 1967.

Hubbart, Marilyn Stall. "Thomas Hardy's Use of Folk Culture in *The Woodlanders.*" *Kentucky Folklore Record* 23 (1977): 17-24.

Humm, Maggie. "Gender and Narrative in Thomas Hardy." *The Thomas Hardy Yearbook* 11 (1984): 41-48.

Humma, John B. "*Sister Carrie* and Thomas Hardy, Regained." *Dreiser Studies* 23.1 (1992): 8-26.

Hyman, Virginia R. *Ethical Perspective in the Novels of Thomas Hardy*. New York: Kennikat Press, 1975.

Ingersoll, Earl G. "Troping and the Machine in Thomas Hardy's *The Mayor of Casterbridge*." *University of Hartford Studies in Literature* 22.2-3 (1996): 59-67.

— — —. "Writing and Memory in *The Mayor of Casterbridge*." *English Literature in Transition* 33.3 (1990): 299-309.

Ingham, Patricia. "The Evolution of *Jude the Obscure*." *The Review of English Studies* 27 (1976): 27-37, 159-169.

Irvin, Glenn. "Structure and Tone in *The Woodlanders*." *Thomas Hardy Annual* 2 (1984): 79-90.

Jackson, Arlene M. *Illustration and the Novels of Thomas Hardy*. Totowa, New Jersey: Rowman and Littlefield, 1981.

Jagdish, Chandra Dave. *The Human Predicament in Hardy's Novels*. London: Macmillan, 1985.

Jedrzejewski, Jan. *Thomas Hardy and the Church*. New York: St. Martin's Press, 1996.

Jewell, John. "Hardy's *The Return of the Native*." *The Explicator* 49.3 (1991): 159-162.

Jones, Lawrence. " 'A Good Hand at a Serial': Thomas Hardy and the Serialization of *Far From the Madding Crowd*." *Studies in the Novel*. 10.3 (1978): 320-334.

— — —. " 'Infected by a Vein of Mimeticism': George Eliot and the Technique of *Far from the Madding Crowd*." *The Journal of Narrative Technique* 8 (1978): 56-76.

Jordan, Mary Ellen. "Thomas Hardy's *The Return of the Native*: Clym Yeobright and Melancholia." *American Imago* 39.2 (1982): 101-118.

Kalikoff, Beth. "The Execution of Tess d'Urberville at Wintoncester." *Executions and the British Experience from the 17th to the 20th Century: A Collection of Essays.* Ed. William D. Thesing. Jefferson: McFarland, 1990. 111-121.

Kelley, Mary Ann. "Individuation and Consummation in Hardy's *Jude the Obscure.*" *The Victorian Newsletter* 82 (1992): 62-64.

Kiely, Robert. "Vision and Viewpoint in *The Mayor of Casterbridge.*" *Nineteenth-Century Fiction* 23.2 (1968): 189-200.

Kramer, Dale. "Character and the Cycle of Change in *The Mayor of Casterbridge.*" *Tennessee Studies in Literature* 16 (1971): 111-120.

— — —. Introduction. *The Woodlanders.* By Thomas Hardy. New York: Oxford University Press, 1985. xi-xxi.

— — —. *Thomas Hardy, The Forms of Tragedy.* Detroit: Wayne State University Press, 1975.

— — —. "Two 'New' Texts of Thomas Hardy's *The Woodlanders.*" *Studies in Bibliography* 20 (1967): 135-150.

— — —, ed. *Critical Approaches to the Fiction of Thomas Hardy.* New York: Macmillan, 1979.

Laird, John T. *The Shaping of "Tess of the d'Urbervilles."* London: Oxford University Press, 1975.

Langbaum, Robert. "The Minimization of Sexuality in *The Mayor of Casterbridge.*" *The Thomas Hardy Journal* 8.1 (1992): 20-32.

— — —. *Thomas Hardy in Our Time.* New York: St. Martin's Press, 1995.

Larson, Dixie Lee. "Eustacia Vye's Drowning: Defiance Versus Convention." *The Thomas Hardy Journal* 9.3 (1993): 55-63.

LaValley, Albert J., ed. *Twentieth-Century Interpretations of "Tess of the d'Urbervilles."* Englewood Cliffs: Prentice Hall, 1969.

Lefebure, Molly. *Thomas Hardy's World: The Life, Times and Works of the Great Novelist and Poet.* London: Carlton Books Limited, 1996.

Lerner, Laurence. *Thomas Hardy's "The Mayor of Casterbridge": Tragedy or Social History?* London: Sussex University Press, 1975.

LeVay, John. "Hardy's *Jude the Obscure*." *The Explicator* 49.4 (1991): 219-222.

Lewis, C. Day, and R. A. Scott-James. *Thomas Hardy.* London: F. Mildner & Sons, 1965.

Lothe, Jakob. "Hardy's Authorial Narrative Method in *Tess of the d'Urbervilles*." *The Nineteenth-Century British Novel.* Ed. Jeremy Hawthorne. Baltimore: Edward Arnold, 1986. 157-170.

Magee, John. "Hardy's *The Return of the Native*." *The Explicator* 53.4 (1995): 216-217.

Mahar, Margaret. "Hardy's Poetry of Renunciation." *English Literary History* 45 (1978): 303-324.

Mallett, Phillip. "Sexual Ideology and Narrative Form in *Jude the Obscure*." *English* 162 (1989): 211-224.

— — —. " 'Smacked, and Brought to Her Senses': Hardy and the Clitheroe Abduction Case." *The Thomas Hardy Journal* 8.2 (1992): 70-73.

May, Charles E. "The Magic of Metaphor in *The Return of the Native*." *The Colby Library Quarterly* 22.2 (1986): 111-118.

McCormack, Peggy A. "The Syntax of Quest in *Jude the Obscure*." *The New Orleans Review* 8.1 (1981): 42-48.

McCullen, J. T., Jr. "Henchard's Sale of Susan in *The Mayor of Casterbridge*." *English Language Notes* 2.3 (1965): 217-218.

McNees, Eleanor. "Reverse Typology in *Jude the Obscure*." *Christianity and Literature* 39.1 (1989): 35-49.

Meisel, Perry. *Thomas Hardy: The Return of the Repressed*. New Haven, CT: Yale University Press, 1972.

Mickelson, Anne Z. "The Family Trap in *The Return of the Native*." *Colby Library Quarterly* 10.8 (1974): 463-475.

Miller, J. Hillis. *Thomas Hardy: Distance and Desire*. Cambridge, MA: Harvard University Press, 1970.

— — —. "Topography in *The Return of the Native*." *Essays in Literature* 8.2 (1981): 119-134.

Millgate, Michael. *Thomas Hardy: A Biography*. New York: Random House, 1982.

— — —. *Thomas Hardy: His Career as a Novelist*. New York: St. Martin's Press, 1994.

— — —, ed. *Letters of Emma and Florence Hardy*. Oxford: Clarendon Press, 1996.

Mistichelli, William. "Androgyny, Survival, and Fulfillment in Thomas Hardy's *Far from the Madding Crowd*." *Modern Language Studies* 28.3 (1988): 53-64.

Mohan, Devinder. "Romanticism and the Woman: A Comparative View of Hawthorne's Hester Prynne, Hardy's Sue Bridehead, Chatterjee's Rohini and Hesse's Kamala." *The Literary Half-Yearly* 27.1 (1986): 78-88.

Moore, Kevin Z. "Death Against Life: Hardy's Mortified and Mortifying 'Man of Character' in *The Mayor of Casterbridge*." *Ball State University Forum* 24.3 (1983): 13-25.

Morgan, Rosemarie. "Passive Victim? *Tess of the d'Urbervilles*." *The Thomas Hardy Journal* 5.1 (1989): 31-54.

Morrison, Ronald D. "Love and Evolution in Thomas Hardy's *The Woodlanders*." *Kentucky Philological Review* 6 (1991): 32-37.

— — —. "Reading and Restoration in *Tess of the d'Urbervilles*." *Victorian Newsletter* 82 (1992): 27-35.

Moses, Michael Valdez. "Agon in the Marketplace: *The Mayor of Casterbridge* as Bourgeois Tragedy." *The South Atlantic Quarterly* 87.2 (1988): 219-151.

Nemesvari, Richard. "Appropriating the Word: *Jude the Obscure* as Subversive Apocrypha." *Victorian Review* 19.2 (1993): 48-66.

Nollen, E. M. "The Loving Look in *Far from the Madding Crowd*." *The Thomas Hardy Yearbook* 13 (1986): 69-73.

Nunokawa, Jeff. "Tess, Tourism, and the Spectacle of the Woman." *Rewriting the Victorians: Theory, History, and the Politics of Gender*. Ed. Linda M. Shires. New York: Routledge, 1992. 70-85.

Orel, Harold. *The Final Years of Thomas Hardy, 1912-1928*. Lawrence: University Press of Kansas, 1976.

— — —. *The Unknown Thomas Hardy: Lesser-Known Aspects of Hardy's Life and Career*. Brighton, East Sussex: Harvester Press, 1987.

— — —, ed. *Thomas Hardy's Personal Writings*. Lawrence: University of Kansas Press, 1996.

Parker, Lynn. " 'Pure Woman' and Tragic Heroine? Conflicting Myths in Hardy's *Tess of the d'Urbervilles*." *Studies in the Novel* 24.3 (1992): 273-280.

Paterson, John. *The Making of "The Return of the Native*." Westport, CT: Greenwood Press, 1978.

Peck, John. "Hardy's *The Woodlanders*: The Too Transparent Web." *English Literature in Transition* 24.3 (1981): 147-154.

Pettit, Charles P. C. "Hardy's Concept of Purity in *Tess of the d'Urbervilles*." *The Thomas Hardy Journal* 7.3 (1991): 48-57.

— — —. "Hardy's Vision of the Individual in *Tess of the d'Urbervilles.*" *New Perspectives on Thomas Hardy.* Ed. Charles P. C. Pettit. New York: St. Martin's Press, 1994. 172-190.

— — —, ed. *Celebrating Thomas Hardy.* New York: St. Martin's Press, 1996.

Pickrel, Paul. "*Jude the Obscure* and the Fall of Phaethon." *Hudson Review* (1986): 231-250.

Pinck, Joan B. "The Reception of Thomas Hardy's *The Return of the Native.*" *Harvard Library Bulletin* 17.3 (1969): 291-308.

Pinion, F. B. "The Country and Period of *The Woodlanders.*" *The Thomas Hardy Yearbook* 2 (1971): 46-55.

— — —. *A Hardy Companion: A Guide to the Works of Thomas Hardy and Their Background.* London: Macmillan, 1968.

— — —. *Thomas Hardy: His Life and Friends.* New York: St. Martin's Press, 1996.

— — —. *A Thomas Hardy Dictionary.* New York: New York University Press, 1989.

Ponsford, Michael. "Thomas Hardy's Control of Sympathy in *Tess of the d'Urbervilles.*" *The Midwest Quarterly* 27.4 (1986): 487-503.

Prentiss, Norman D. "The Tortured Form of *Jude the Obscure.*" *Colby Quarterly* 31.3 (1995): 179-193.

Purdy, Richard L. *Thomas Hardy: A Bibliographical Study.* Oxford: Clarendon Press, 1968.

Pyle, Forest. "Demands of History: Narrative Crisis in *Jude the Obscure.*" *New Literary History* 26.2 (1995): 359-378.

Raine, Craig. "Conscious Artistry in *The Mayor of Casterbridge.*" *New Perspectives on Thomas Hardy.* Ed. Charles P. C. Pettit. New York: St. Martin's Press, 1994. 156-171.

Ray, Martin. "Hardy's Borrowing from Shakespeare: Eustacia Vye and Lady Macbeth." *The Thomas Hardy Yearbook* 14 (1987): 64.

Reid, Fred. "Art and Ideology in *Far from the Madding Crowd.*" *Thomas Hardy Annual* 4 (1986): 91-126.

Renner, Stanley. "Mary Teller and Sue Bridehead: Birds of a Feather in 'The White Quail' and *Jude the Obscure.*" *Steinbeck Quarterly* 18.1-2 (1985): 35-45.

Rutland, William R. *Thomas Hardy: A Study of His Writings and Their Background.* New York: Russell & Russell, 1962.

Sasaki, Toru. "On Boldwood's Retina: A 'Moment of Vision' in *Far from the Madding Crowd* and Its Possible Relation to *Middlemarch.*" *The Thomas Hardy Journal* 8 (1992): 57-60.

Saxelby, Outwin F. *A Thomas Hardy Dictionary.* New York: Humanities Press, 1962.

Schweik, Robert C. "Character and Fate in Hardy's *Mayor of Casterbridge.*" *Nineteenth-Century Fiction* 21 (1966): 249-262.

— — —. "The Early Development of Hardy's *Far From the Madding Crowd.*" *Texas Studies in Literature and Language* 9 (1967): 414-428.

— — —. "An Error in the Text of Hardy's *Far from the Madding Crowd.*" *Colby Library Quarterly* VII.6 (1966): 269.

— — —. "A First Draft Chapter of Hardy's *Far from the Madding Crowd.*" *English Studies* 53 (1972): 344-349.

— — —. "The Narrative Structure of *Far from the Madding Crowd.*" *Budmouth Essays on Thomas Hardy.* Ed. F. B. Pinion. Dorchester: The Thomas Hardy Society, 1976. 21-38.

Seymour-Smith, Martin. *Hardy: A Biography.* New York: St. Martin's Press, 1994.

Shelston, Alan. "The Particular Pleasure of *Far from the Madding Crowd*." *The Thomas Hardy Yearbook* 7 (1977): 31-39.

—— ——. " 'Were they Beautiful?': *Far from the Madding Crowd* and *Daniel Deronda*." *The Thomas Hardy Journal* 81 (1992): 65-67.

Shires, Linda M. "Narrative, Gender, and Power in *Far from the Madding Crowd*." *The Sense of Sex.* Ed. Margaret R. Higonnet. Chicago: University of Illinois Press, 1993. 49-65.

Silverman, Kaja. "History, Figuration and Female Subjectivity in *Tess of the d'Urbervilles*." *Novel* 18.1 (1984): 4-28.

Simpson, Anne B. "Sue Bridehead Revisited." *Victorian Literature and Culture* 19 (1991): 55-66.

Skilling, M. R. "Investigation into the Country of *The Woodlanders*." *The Thomas Hardy Journal* 8.3 (1992): 62-67.

Smith, J. B. " 'Bees up Flues' and 'Chips in Porridge' : Two Proverbial Sayings in Thomas Hardy's *The Return of the Native*." *Proverbium* 12 (1995): 315-322.

Sommers, Jeffrey. "Hardy's Other Bildungsroman: *Tess of the d'Urbervilles*." *English Literature in Transition, 1880-1920* 25 (1982): 159-168.

Southerington, F. R. "Thomas Hardy in *Jude the Obscure*." *The Thomas Hardy Yearbook* 1 (1970): 62-69.

Springer, Marlene. *Hardy's Use of Allusion.* Lawrence: University Press of Kansas, 1983.

Squillace, Robert. "Hardy's Mummers." *Nineteenth-Century Literature* 41.2 (1986): 172-189.

Squires, Michael. "*Far from the Madding Crowd* as Modified Pastoral" *Nineteenth-Century Fiction* 25.3 (1970): 299-326.

Stevens, Jack. "Literary and Biographical Allusion in *Tess of the d'Urbervilles*." *The Thomas Hardy Yearbook* 14 (1987): 20-25.

Stottlar, James F. "Hardy vs. Pinero: Two Stage Versions of *Far from the Madding Crowd*." *Theatre Survey* 28.2 (1977): 23-43.

Stout, Janis P. "The Fallen Woman and the Conflicted Author: Hawthorne and Hardy." *American Transcendental Quarterly* 1.3 (1987): 233-246.

Sumner, Rosemary. *Thomas Hardy: Psychological Novelist.* New York: St. Martin's Press, 1981.

Sutherland, J. A. *Victorian Novelists and Publishers.* Chicago: University of Chicago Press, 1976.

Swann, Charles. "*Far from the Madding Crowd*: How Good a Shepherd is Gabriel Oak?" *Notes and Queries* 39.2 (1992): 17.

— — —. "A Hardy Debt to Hawthorne." *Notes and Queries* 6 (1992): 188-189.

Taft, Michael. "Hardy's Manipulation of Folklore and Literary Imagination: The Case of the Wife-Sale in *The Mayor of Casterbridge*." *Studies in the Novel* 13.4 (1981): 399-407.

Taylor, Dennis. *Hardy's Literary Language and Victorian Philology.* Oxford: Clarendon Press, 1993.

Taylor, Richard H., ed. *The Personal Notebooks of Thomas Hardy.* New York: Columbia University Press, 1979.

Temple, Ruth Z., and Martin Tuclar, eds. *A Library of Literary Criticism: Modern British Literature.* Volume II. New York: Frederick Ungar Publishing Co., 1977.

Thesing, William B. " 'The Question of Matrimonial Divergence': Distorting Mirrors and Windows in Hardy's *The Woodlanders*." *The Thomas Hardy Yearbook* 14 (1987): 44-52.

Trezise, Simon. "Ways of Learning in *The Return of the Native*." *The Thomas Hardy Journal* 7.2 (1991): 56-65.

Vandiver, Edward P. "*The Return of the Native* and Shakespeare." *Furman Studies* 12.1 (1964): 11-15.

Veidemanis, Gladys V. "*Tess of the d'Urbervilles*: What the Film Left Out." *The English Journal* 77.7 (1988): 53-57.

Viera, Carroll. "The Name Levi in *Far from the Madding Crowd*." *The Thomas Hardy Yearbook* 14 (1987): 63.

Vigar, Penelope. *The Novels of Thomas Hardy: Illusion and Reality*. London: The Althlone Press, 1974.

Wasserman, Julian N. "A Note on the Church of St. Thomas in *Jude the Obscure*." *The Thomas Hardy Yearbook* 14 (1987): 9-12.

Watts, Cedric. "Hardy's Sue Bridehead and the 'New Woman.' " *Critical Survey* 5.2 (1993): 152-156.

Weber, Carl J., comp. *The First Hundred Years of Thomas Hardy 1840-1940: A Centenary Bibliography of Hardiana*. Waterville: Colby College Library, 1942.

Webster, Roger. "Reproducing Hardy: Familiar and Unfamiliar Versions of *Far from the Madding Crowd* and *Tess of the d'Urbervilles*." *Critical Survey* 5.2 (1993): 143-151.

Welsh, James M. "Hardy and the Pastoral, Schlesinger and Shepherds: *Far from the Madding Crowd*." *Literature and Film Quarterly* 9.2 (1981): 79-84.

Wickens, G. Glenn. "'Sermons in Stones': The Return to Nature in *Tess of the d'Urbervilles*." *English Studies in Canada* 14.2 (1988): 184-203.

Widdowson, Peter. *Thomas Hardy*. Plymouth, OK: Northcote House, 1996.

Wilson, Keith. *Thomas Hardy on Stage*. New York: St. Martin's Press, 1995.

Windram, William T. "A Discrepancy in *Far from the Madding Crowd*." *Notes and Queries* 29.4 (1982): 326.

Winfield, Christine. "The Manuscript of Hardy's *Mayor of Casterbridge*." *The Papers of the Bibliographical Society of America* 67 (1973): 33-58.

Wittenburg, Judith Bryant. "Angles of Vision and Questions of Gender in *Far from the Madding Crowd*." *The Centennial Review* 30 (1986): 25-40.

Wotton, George. *Thomas Hardy: Towards a Materialist Criticism*. Totowa, New Jersey: Gill & Macmillan, 1985.

Wright, Reg., ed. *Two English Masters: Charles Dickens and Thomas Hardy*. New York: Marshall Cavendish, 1989.

Wright, Terence. *Tess of the d'Urbervilles*. London: Macmillan, 1987.

Wyatt, Bryant N. "Poetic Justice in *The Return of the Native*." *Mark Twain Journal* 21.4 (1983): 56-57.

Zellefrow, Ken. "*The Return of the Native*: Hardy's Map and Eustacia's Suicide." *Nineteenth-Century Fiction* 28.2 (1973): 214-221.

About the Author

Julie Sherrick first became interested in the works of Thomas Hardy during her graduate studies at St. Bonaventure University. Since that time, she has had the opportunity to visit Dorset and to present a public lecture on Thomas Hardy at Somerville College in Oxford. Throughout the past decade, Professor Sherrick has served as a curriculum consultant, English teacher, and an ESL teacher. In addition, she has had numerous opportunities to address her peers on matters relating to curriculum and instruction, and she continues to be actively involved in creating educational materials for the middle-level student. Presently, Professor Sherrick is a middle school teacher in southwestern New York State and an adjunct lecturer at St. Bonaventure University.